Euripides
The Bacchae

TRANSLATED

BY

HERBERT GOLDER

Euripides *The Bacchae*, Translated and with an Introduction by Herbert Golder © 2001

Library of Congress Catalog-in-Publication Data

Euripides.
  [Bacchae. English]
  The Bacchae/translated by Herbert Golder.
  p.cm.
  ISBN 1-55783-445-8
  1. Pentheus (Greek mythology--Drama. 2. Dionysus (Greek deity)
--Drama. 3. Bacchantes--Drama. I. Golder, Herbert. II. Title

PA3975.B2 G65 2001
882'.01-dc21   2001046097

Jacket Photograph: Courtesy of Kimbell Art Museum, Fort Worth, Texas
Detail of AP 2000.2, Greek, Early Classical period, Attributed to Douris as painter & Python as potter, **Red-Figure Cup Showing Death of Pentheus**, Terra-cotta, c. 480 B.C. 5 h. x 11 1/2 in. diameter (12. 7 h x 29.2 cm diameter)
Photographer Michael Bodycomb 2000

Applause Theatre & Cinema Books
151 West 46th Street, 8th Floor,
New York, New York 10036
Phone: 212-575-9265
Fax: 646-562-5852

Sales & Distribution
Hal Leonard Corporation
7777 West Bluemound Road
P O Box 13819
Milwaukee, WI 53213
1-800-524-4425

Euripides
The Bacchae

TRANSLATED

BY

HERBERT GOLDER

To the maenads ...

INTRODUCTION

1. Euripides and Dionysos

Euripides was over seventy when he wrote *The Bacchae*, a prolific playwright who had won few prizes; according to tradition, he began writing plays at eighteen, received a chorus only when he was thirty, and did not win first prize at the annual competition in Athens until the age of forty-four. His unconventional style, musical innovations, intellectually chic language, and often shockingly erotic subjects had made him the butt of the comedians; his indictments of imperialism, warmongering, and demagoguery must have caused resentment. In 408 he left the cosmopolitan but increasingly corrupt world of Athens for more primitive Macedonia, in what was perhaps the self-imposed exile of a disillusioned man. By the winter of 407/406 he had died. *The Bacchae* was found among his "things": staged the following year by his son, the younger Euripides, the play earned its author the first prize that had so often eluded him.

Euripides was admired for his technical virtuosity, his "special effects" (like his spectacular use of the *deus ex machina*), and memorable songs (according to Plutarch, Athenian sailors were released by their Syracusan captors if they could sing Euripidean lyrics). His contemporaries were often dazzled by the Dionysiac surface of his drama: his more colloquial rhythms, his new "Asiatic" music, astrophic lyrics, the cleverness and spoken *détente* of his dialogue, his psychically fragmented characters, and their heightened emotionality. What they could not — or would not — see was that the style reflected their own obsessions no less than the poet's. Impressed by illusionistic invention, they were often blind to his tragic vision: his lifelong effort to compel his audience to accept an *anagnorisis*, a recognition of themselves and their cultural and spiritual impasse. In *The Frogs* Aristophanes has Dionysos bring Aeschylus, not Euripides, back from Hades to save Athens.

The Bacchae plays out a crisis of man and god and uses the theater reflexively as an arena, Dionysos' own, in which this larger drama can be enacted. But the play is not, primarily, a self-conscious exploration of the limits of theatrical illusion; nor is Dionysos, as god of theater, merely Euripides' occupational patron deity. Dionysos is the god of theater because, like the theater and its symbol, the mask, he mediates orders of reality — the familiar and the mysterious, the ephemeral and the eternal, the terrible and the beautiful, the immanent and the transcendent. He is what Plato termed a *daimon*. To lose Dionysos is to lose the transforming power of imagination itself.

Art presents lies that show the truth. Or, in the words of Gorgias, Euripides' contemporary, "By its myths and passions tragedy creates that deception in respect to which he who deceives is more in the right than he who does not deceive, and he who is deceived is wiser than he who is not deceived." A famous fresco at Pompeii depicts two boys and a mask: one boy raises a silver bowl to his lips; on its concave inner surface he sees reflected a mask of the paternal satyr, Silenus, which the other boy holds up behind his head. The optical illusion allows the boy to see himself as the more potent being he is about to become. Before appearing on stage, an actor in a Noh play enters a "mirror room," where he stares at his own reflection and then turns to meditate upon his mask. One must turn from the mirror to the mask, from the familiar reflection of oneself to the emergent "other." To those who can see, the mask reveals a deeper truth; for those who cannot, it is at best a diversion, at worst a delusion. Euripides' Dionysos emerges as the consummate master of theatrical artifice who runs through the full gamut of his powers (from costume change to earthquake) to destroy a society that has ceased to face or understand complex truths about itself, and now must suffer visionary illusion as bewildering delusion.

Dionysos *was* a real god, and his cult probably did come from the East to Greece, though in a time remembered by Euripides' audience only as mythic. At its most intense, his religion was a mystery religion which promised its devotee spiritual renewal. Vase paintings of the period show us how the poet's contemporaries liked to imagine the orgiastic worship of Dionysos. A young animal, the god's surrogate, was dismembered alive and eaten while its flesh was still warm and bleeding. Transported by this rite and by the god's ecstatic dances, the devotee became fused in body and spirit with the god. Dionysos was, to be sure, a fertility god whose worship was identified with that of Eros and Aphrodite, with Demeter and the season-rhythmed world of nature. But it was in certain plants (like the "warm" vine and the "cool" ivy) and certain animals (like the fawn and the lion) that he manifested his contradictory nature — sometimes gentle, sometimes terrible. He chose those living things whose sap, or blood, contained what Walter Otto called "a mysteriously aroused element of life." He could be felt, for instance, in wine, as its liquid fire warmed the blood. Called, because of his miraculous double birth, the "twice-born" god, he similarly exalted those who experienced him. But the price for the "new life" he conferred was always abandonment of the old. And his vital mysteries therefore required sacrifice and violence.

A healthy world can accommodate, and would in fact require, the life-energy of such a god. But the corollary is perhaps even more apt: a world that cannot accommodate such a god cannot be healthy. To explore the violence on the other side of Dionysos' tame persona of wine-god is to look into the darker mystery that is also part of his divine nature — and of human nature — but that Athens experienced now only in blindness. The play unmasks a savage human truth that lurks behind the palatably Attic, anthropomorphized god. His violence explodes with the force of something that has been suppressed or forgotten: a truth about human life that stays hidden until some extreme crisis necessitates its eruption.

2. Thebes

Indeed, Thebes is like a dormant volcano, suddenly awakened by Dionysos. The sisters of his mother Semele regard the story of the god's miraculous birth as a lie, and behind their skepticism lies the cynicism of the age. That a miracle could come from a union of human and divine is utterly beyond them. This is the kind of world the sisters represent, and why the god they have rejected gives them the only divine experience they would understand — punishment and suffering.

Kadmos and Teiresias are of a piece with these Theban women. Teiresias' argument in favor of the god is merely rationalizing theology. More professional priest than prophet, he sees, and tries to grasp, an opportunity. His sophistic aetiology of the Dionysos myth (arising from a confusion of the word "shone" with "sown") is antithetical to the purity of religious feeling the god's worship requires. His view of divinity is essentially functional and his conceptualization of the gods into abstract principles of wet (Dionysos) and dry (Demeter) resembles nothing so much as the characteristic binaries of both pre-Socratics and sophists — the all-too-confident rationalism of taking things apart and getting things done. No glimmer of the god's ecstatic power appears in the old priest's catechism. And Kadmos, the ancient dynast, sees personal and political opportunity in the new god and his strange story. Even if the story is a lie, he says, it is a useful one. The two of them make the most improbable of votaries of this Dionysos: Who could better embody the loss of Dionysiac vitality than a blind old sophist-seer and a canny ex-king? Barely able to stand erect, the two ancient mummers cut pathetic, even slightly comic, figures as they dodder in Bacchic regalia across the stage, debating whether to ascend the sacred mountain on foot or by coach. The god and his revels have entered the profoundly enfeebled world that these old men, sapped in spirit, canny in mind, embody.

As in so many Euripidean plays, there is a fatal split here between mind and heart. The old men are interested parties in their merely nominal and opportunistic deference to the new god. The chorus of Asian Bacchants, in contrast, is wholly devoted to Dionysos and (it seems reasonable to suppose) expresses that devotion with a choreographic rapture in keeping with the hymnic power and purity of their lyrics. While the two shaky old men rationalize this new religion in a parody of spiritual need, the chorus' genuine religious passion finds convincing expression in the unified ecstatic transports of their bodies. But they are creatures of the god; and they become, in the course of the play, not only his ecstatic dancers but the persuasive mouthpiece of his sensible-sounding morality. In their elation, they make that look elevated which, in reality, subverts all true morality.

And there are also the women on the mountain, enjoying, it seems, the pleasures of a paradise; but they too are actually only the god's prisoners and, finally, the agents of his savage justice. They may seem rapt, but they are in fact true maenads — meaning etymologically women *maddened* by the god. Beast and god merge in them to destroy the human. Dissociation of sensibility, usually represented by polarized characters, is extremely common in late Euripidean drama and reflects the psychic fragmentation of a society whose intelligence has degenerated into cunning which serves rather than controls the passions. The grisly image at the end of the play — the head of Pentheus held up over his shattered body — emblematizes this fatal split. Dramatic and theatrical convention may have required Euripides to present a mythical story in a pre-historical Thebes, but morally the city he depicts is the Athens of the late fifth century, the city suffering from every kind of excess.

3. Pentheus

The play is the existential tragedy of Pentheus as much as the dramatization of a culture in crisis. Pentheus' tragedy is framed by that of the world around him. He enters, tilting as it were, in a world already tilted. His story might have had different consequences, even were his destiny the same, in a world better able to suffer contradictions. But his tragedy is nonetheless paradigmatic in its scope and significance.

In order to put Pentheus prominently into relief, Euripides has altered the story of the reception traditionally given Dionysos as wandering god. It is normally the community as a whole which resists his coming, and only a provident individual, like the helmsman in the Homeric *Hymn to Dionysos*, who recognizes his godhead. Here only Pentheus resists the new god, and acceptance of his worship takes the form of collective madness. The moral order has been reversed precisely in relation to the division of mind and heart. Pentheus, isolated but individuated, is the sole resister, although his own Dionysiac vehemence will wear down his resistance — and his reason. Yet there is more to his violent rejection of the god than his adolescent priggishness or authoritarian temperament. His lone stand against the god is not merely a new twist to the old tale of Dionysos' unwelcome arrival, but the introduction of a new complexity into the myth of Dionysos.

Disarmingly effeminate in appearance, gently submissive to the guards and Pentheus in the "captive" scene, the source of the chorus' rapture, Dionysos seems unjustly attacked by the stubborn young king who opposes him. How can it be right to resist so seductive a divinity? At first, it is true, Pentheus seems a representative of repressive institutions. But after the earthquake we begin to feel slightly uneasy with this playful god as he steps, still sweetly smiling, through the rubble. And when he is unable to talk Pentheus into submission in staccato, single-line exchanges, the god resorts to subterfuge. He emits an eerie sound (AAAAAAAAAH) followed by the question, "Would you like to see them, huddled up there, / on the mountain?" Pentheus: "*See?* I'd give much gold to see that sight." And the contest is suddenly over. Dionysos toys a little with his victim as he costumes him for the slaughter. The little "play" he stages turns into a savage rite of human sacrifice. Pentheus is not even allowed the dignity of an heroic struggle, or for that matter, the dignity of tragedy. The scene in which Pentheus is dressed in woman's garb is not merely comic; it is, in its context, a travesty of the tragic. Dionysos makes his victim a laughingstock, and his own smile turns mocking and sinister. He unmans Pentheus with comedy, then "unmasks" him with tragedy all the more atrocious. Why is the dramatist engaged in this effort to shift our sympathies from Dionysos to Pentheus? How can it be right to resist Dionysos, to challenge a *god*?

Pentheus is right to resist because the world is already, like his own adolescent body, totally in Dionysos' power. The chorus characterizes him as a man of excess, *perissos*, a quality shared by great heroes and great criminals alike, those who do, whether for good or evil, what has never been dared. And Pentheus is not simply overstepping what, in a more static metaphysical scheme, would be his "human limits": he is, though we do not realize this until the play's end, waging war on a beast-god in the ancient heroic tradition. An example will be helpful: in Aeschylus' fragmentary *Bassarids*, Orpheus worships Apollo but refuses to recognize Dionysos. In punishment for what seems to be an act of *hybris* Dionysos drives the woman followers of Orpheus mad and they tear him to pieces, not unlike what happens to Pentheus here. But Orpheus' own mother is not among those who kill him; nor is the divine nature of Dionysos' godhead at issue. In *The Bacchae*, however, the smiling god not only avenges the wrong done him, but does so with a sinister relish that turns savage, as his animal epithets, especially from the middle of the play on, declare. And Pentheus is no Orpheus, a man whose power was so great and whose music so sweet that he was able to pass through the Gates of Death — an heroic feat also accomplished in Greek myth *only* by Herakles. And so, given the odds against him, Pentheus *is* a fool to do battle with this god. But he is also in the right, since he is the only man who still possesses both anything resembling the civic instinct and the courage to resist this monstrous presence that threatens to plunge his entire city into madness and chaos. In a moral order so out of balance, resistance to divine authority appears the only morally right act.

Euripides' protagonists are often adolescents. He uses them the way he uses women: their psychic nakedness makes them different from mature men, who are more distanced from their own natures by socialization and their culturally defined roles. Women and youths make better filters of reality, suffering the passion suffered by the species as a whole, but more vividly.[1] And Pentheus is a typical Euripidean adolescent, like Hippolytus or Ion, desperately trying to hold onto some ordering ideal against a daimonic force, which is irresistible because it is his own, as yet unrecognized, nature. Pentheus is destined to suffer the explosive force of his own opposed needs, and to realize the meaning etymologically present in his own name, *penthos* ("grief," "suffering," "sorrow"). Not just etymology but genealogy too conspires against him. Dionysos taunts him, "You do not know / what you do, nor who you are, / nor why you live." Pentheus responds defiantly, "I am Pentheus, / born of Agave and Echion!" But Pentheus' father Echion, the "Snake-Man," was one of the sown-men of Kadmos; he emerged from the earth, sprung from the dragon's tooth. The snake — or "dragon" — is one of Dionysos' own creatures, symbol of his regenerative potency and sexual ambiguity. Dragonish, chthonic powers generated the blood-violence of this passionate Pentheus. Now they claim him. His tragedy is the generic human tragedy; and, like so many other Euripidean characters, he is inevitably torn to pieces because the skills that might have obviated the tragedy, the ability to mediate extremes, do not exist.

4. Dionysos' Theater of Cruelty

Dionysos never reveals himself to his maenads. He plays with them as he plays with others, for instance, in his banter with them after the earthquake. In fact, he controls every action of the play, up to the entrance of Agave. He elicits choral lyrics which make him seem a god of joy, conferring bliss upon the chaste and humble. But all this is his manipulation of illusion. Dionysos, master of his medium, mesmerizes Pentheus and the spectator with all the representational resources of the theater. He traps his victim with illusion and impersonation. Not merely because he is the god of the theater, but because a masked theater depends on the vitality of the mythmaking imagination. From the first, Dionysos presents himself as a theatrical god, twice telling us that, although he has assumed a mortal shape, he goes disguised. His mask is twice described (no other Greek play directly refers to masks). So the play is, as many critics have noted, extremely "meta-theatrical" — which is not to say the play is chiefly "about" the expressive resources of the theater, but that it exhibits an unusually heightened sense of its own theatricality. Consider, for example, the number of verbal presentations of off-stage events. There are two formal messenger speeches and two highly evocative vignettes, one by the guard, one by Dionysos himself, who contrives his own messenger speech after the earthquake. By verbal means, he re-presents the earthquake he himself has caused, and which the spectator (as well as the Chorus) has just experienced as theatrical mirage. Characteristic of the graphic messenger-type speech so often used to represent off-stage prodigies are heightened sonority, rhetorical elevation, but above all appeals to the visual faculty (vivid accounts of off-stage events, descriptions of the act of seeing itself, verbs of looking, invitations to imagine the spectacle, allusions to the sun's radiance, bright reflections, or fire); all these combine synesthetically to make the unseen visible. No other play is so rich in this kind of illusionistic representation of off-stage events. By presenting his actual earth-shaking power as stylized illusion, he collapses the ordinary boundaries of illusion and reality. And, in one way or another, Dionysos clearly controls the representation of his miracles, all designed to lure Pentheus to the mountain to *see* what should *not* be seen: *the forbidden mystery*.

It is, in fact, just this aspect of illusionistic representation to which Euripides draws our attention with Pentheus' brusque interruption of the messenger ("Is your message urgent?"). More is at stake than an amusing piece of stage business. Pentheus is disallowing a mimetic mode, expressed through the evocative exaggerations of the Messenger speech. At its best, the cult of Dionysos employs madness in order to create insight; his theater uses illusion to reveal truth. Pentheus, though, remains unmoved by the Messenger's account, by the Guard's vivid narrative, and even by the earthquake, mistrusting what he hears and sees as conjurer's tricks.

Pentheus rejects the mask's duality, epitomized by the messenger's account of the unseen. The scene in which Dionysos dresses the young king in woman's clothes effectively dramatizes Pentheus' fatal inability to "mask." The clumsiness with which Pentheus assumes that improbable part invites both pity and derision. But the laughter quickly fades as the tragic momentum builds. Beside the smiling, androgynous god stands the absurdly costumed Pentheus, turning around on tiptoe, adjusting his hem. At this moment, Pentheus must look uncannily like Dionysos himself — like, in fact, the god's theatrical double. What differentiates them — apart from the grace of the one and the awkwardness of the other — are their respective masks. Dionysos' impassive smile now turns mocking; by contrast, Pentheus' traditional unsmiling tragic mask must seem to wear an expression of horror. Thus, paradoxically, at the very moment of their closest likeness, the two worlds of divine and human could not appear further apart.

Dionysos has trapped Pentheus in the theater-world of mask and illusion, a realm where Pentheus is bound, given his rigid character, to lose himself. To play so uncharacteristic a part requires a fluidity of imagination that Pentheus lacks. Instead of the clarity that the doubling mirror of theatrical illusion can produce, he sees only the blurred image of his original one-dimensional world. The two Thebes of Pentheus' delusion are the emblem of a dissociated sensibility, of a consciousness that maintains dream-world and day-world, fantasy and reality, fiction and fact as entirely separate realms. A man so unused to imaginative exertion is all the more quickly and easily overcome by it.

"Every profound mind," Nietzsche wrote, "needs a mask." Masks invoke presences but also preserve distance: Even among peoples whose religions involve masked dancing, ritual taboos protect the impersonator from the mask. Pentheus has "stepped" too far into his mask, which is, in effect, the same as not wearing one. Unlike the Noh actor, Pentheus cannot turn from the mirror to the mask — cannot, in other words, expand the self into the guise of another. Pentheus' mask merely blinds him to who he is, and so he assumes his new part with such dangerously Dionysian abandon that he loses himself altogether within it.

The man who spies is spied upon; the predator very soon becomes the prey. Pentheus and the "Stranger" went to Kithairon, as the Messenger says, "hoping to see without being seen." Instead, "they saw him, the Maenads, and not he them." Pentheus undergoes an optical reversal through which he is denied sight and suffers instead the blinding force of his own nature. He cannot play his spectator's part, like one who sees the truth *in*, and *through*, the looking glass of Dionysian illusion, because he hasn't the "art" of seeing. He comes instead to *spy* on the women and to *expose* the god's mysteries. Because he denies the god and the god's gift of truth-through-illusion, Pentheus succeeds only in making a tragic "spectacle" of himself.

Pentheus can not experience the god's illusions except as delusion. The god whose divinity he denies reverts to some dragonish thing, and his theater slides backwards into a primitive rite of human sacrifice. The head/mask of Pentheus held up by Agave at the end of the play is, on the one hand, primitive horror — masks daubed with blood and hung from trees were used in primitive Dionysian cult — and, on the other, a complex symbol. In a play so self-reflexively "theatrical" there is no evading the portent of that dangling mask. The theater, as one of Athens' civilizing institutions, has been reduced to a *trompe l'oeil* artifice, a mask without a man, a disembodied convention. Pentheus is the scapegoat for a society that had lost its capacity to comprehend the complex contradictions of their own Dionysian natures. In the end, the tutelary god of Athens' greatest instrument of culture, the theater, returns here to deliver a *coup de grace* to this spiritually exhausted society. Shortly after this play was produced, tragedy itself would effectively die as an art form. Like Pentheus, Athens had lost its ability to assume — what Yeats once identified as the source of all human happiness — "the mask of some other life."

5. Survivors

But the play does not end with the gory spectacle of Pentheus' severed head. Something happens to suggest that the human spirit possesses a strength equal to the vulnerability of the body. The scene in which Kadmos brings Agave back to sanity is the theatrical reverse of the earlier one when Dionysos promised Pentheus marvelous sights, then took away his ability to see. Here Kadmos restores his god-intoxicated daughter to true, albeit tragic, sight. The scene dramatizes the agony — but also the "art" — of seeing. Euripides signals this with a vivid account of the *act of seeing* itself. Kadmos instructs Agave to turn her eyes — eyes that previously rolled with madness — towards the ether. Suddenly, everything seems clearer. "On your marriage day," Kadmos now asks, "to whom did I give you?" "To Echion," she replies, "a man, they say, who sprang from the dragon's tooth." The woman who earlier used snakes to girdle her fawnskin is now astonished by the strange story of Echion's autochthony. She discovers who she is, to what she was bound, what she has wrought. The play, and our sympathies, is turning against Dionysos at the very moment that his victory is crowned.

Kadmos goes further still. He makes Agave herself declare the worst part about the truth she is about to see. This is not maudlin melodrama but the dynamic of revelation — from sound to sight, from verbal to visual meaning —

by which the dark truth is brought to light in Greek tragedy. Agave must *say* it, before she will be able to *see*, and *see* so as to *know* it. The verb "to know" in Greek is, literally, "to have seen," that is, *seeing* in the perfect tense — "perfected" sight. So, Kadmos forces her to say that Pentheus is *her* son, conceived in union with her husband, Echion, the Snake-Man. The horror she holds in her hands is, in both biological and moral terms, *truly her own*. She is being verbally "prepared" for tragic vision. It is unmistakably the head of Pentheus she holds, and to which she must now turn her eyes. With "ethereal" clarity she sees the blood on her own hands. The visually significant moment, the moment of seeing itself, is verbally marked. She declares the thing she sees and the spectacle she now embodies. A maenad no longer mad, she confronts a mask no longer manned: a head torn from its body, the body of feeling divorced from its mind — tragic emblem of a society in disintegration, of cultural *sparagmos*.

Agave proceeds to reassemble in spirit, restoring the head to the body, what the god has shattered in the flesh. If the scene with Agave and the mask represents the ultimate triumph of this savage god who now presides over a primitive sacrifice, then the scene in which Kadmos has coaxed his daughter away from the god's delusion, and in which she now mourns her son's body and restores his head, represents an effort to piece back together, with nothing more than love and resilience of spirit, the life that the god has torn apart. It is their dramatization of human affection and devotion that alone heals. When the monstrous god appears, it is hard to imagine that he still wears his smiling disguise. Now we see him as he is, what Pentheus resisted all along: the beast. The chorus' final cry for vengeance invoked Dionysos as snake, bull, and lion. Now, wearing the mask of the beast, as one or as some hybrid of these creatures, he appears to gloat over his savage justice and to transform Kadmos back into the serpent from which the human city arose. But in spite of this apocalyptic vision, and the god's impatience with their delay, the scene of human tenderness continues as Kadmos and Agave embrace. Kadmos has denounced the god's "justice"; Agave will forswear his rites. A sense of what ultimately unites human beings emerges. Their protracted farewell is a refusal of atrocity and turns the play into a human tragedy in spite of the beast-cum-god overhead.[2]

NOTES

[1] An observation I owe, along with much else in this essay, to the late William Arrowsmith, and which is developed more fully in his forthcoming "Euripides and the Dramaturgy of Crisis." A very special debt of gratitude is owed to William Arrowsmith who read and commented on an earlier version of this essay and who first encouraged me to attempt a translation of *The Bacchae*, a work which I had myself first experienced in his own brilliant version, and from whom I learned more about Euripides and a good deal else than words can ever express.

[2] I am grateful to my colleagues John Carlevale and Nicholas Poburko for reading and commenting on various drafts of this introduction.

CHARACTERS

DIONYSOS
(also called BROMIOS, EVIUS,
and BACCHUS)

CHORUS OF ASIAN BACCHAE
(followers of Dionysos)

TEIRESIAS

KADMOS

PENTHEUS

ATTENDANTS

FIRST MESSENGER

SECOND MESSENGER

AGAVE

CHORUS LEADER

The royal palace of Thebes.

Before it, the vine-covered ruins of a smoldering tomb, that of Semele, mother of Dionysos.
On the left, the road to the city; on the right, the road to the mountain, Kithairon.

The god DIONYSOS *enters from the right. He is dressed as a Bacchant, one of his own adepts. He wears a fawnskin and carries a thyrsos, a long stalk of fennel tipped with clusters of ivy. He is very young, with long, light hair. He wears a smiling mask.*

DIONYSOS
I am Dionysos! Son of Zeus I have come
to this land of Thebes where I was born
in a blaze, the lightning-labor of Semele,
child of Kadmos. A god in the shape of a man
I come to the springs of Dirke and streams of Ismenus.
There before the palace lies my mother's tomb,
all that remains of her marriage to the lightning of Zeus,
these smoking ruins and flames that live
forever within this shrine of hatred everlasting —
Hera's deathless rage against my mother.
Kadmus I praise, he made this place sacred to his daughter,
a shrine where none may tread. But it was I,
I who entwined this place with thick green clusters
and smothered it with vines.
      Behind me lie lands rich in gold — Lydia, Phrygia.
And I have crossed the steppes of Persia,
under a sun that beats forever down; I have passed
through Baktria's walled cities, and travelled
over Media's icy wastes; I have been to splendid Arabia,
and the Asian coast, where Greeks and Barbarians mix
in teeming, towering cities that meet the sea.

In all these places I have taught my mysteries
and laid down my rites, to be revealed
on earth — for what I am: god.
    Now here, in Thebes, here before anywhere else in Greece,
I have raised my cry:

      anololuxa!

Theban women wear my fawnskin now against their flesh
and carry my thyrsos in their hands — my thyrsos,
my holy ivy-covered spear. But why here, why Thebes?
I come to refute the slander against my mother,
the slander by her sisters — her sisters!
They who should have been the last to do this:
to deny that I am Dionysos, god, born of Zeus,
and say my father was mortal,
some man Semele took into her bed,
and then, to hide her shame, blamed me on Zeus,
my birth a fraud, they claim, contrived by Kadmos!
And for *her* blasphemous lie, they sneer,
Zeus blasted her with his lightning.
But for *their* outrage I drive these women from their homes,
hound them with madness to the mountain, where they rave
completely in my power. Now by force they wear my costume
and carry the trappings of my rites.
Yes, every last woman of Kadmos' race is there,
gone to the mountain wholly in my thrall.
There the daughters of Kadmos sprawl under green firs
and crouch against bare rock.
    Like it or not, this city must learn its lesson:
what it means to disbelieve my mysteries.
I will vindicate my mother: I will reveal myself,
mortals will see me for the god she bore to Zeus.

    As for Kadmos, he has grown old and given his power
to Pentheus, his grandson, who now makes this war on god
in me and drives me from libations and forgets my name in prayers.

But for *his* outrage, I will show him, show him and every son of Thebes,
that I am god born.
          And when I have settled matters here,
I will set off for other lands and there too
reveal my godhead. But should this city dare
remove my Bacchants from the mountain by a show of might,
I will lead an army of Maenads against it.
For this, you see, I have shed my godlike form
and assumed man's nature in a mortal shape.
          But now enough. Come to me, my troupe, my throng of dancers!
Together we have travelled far, over Tmolos I have led you,
out of Lydia, far from barbarian lands.
Now bring your Phrygian drums — your gift from me and mother Rhea —
and pound the gates of Pentheus' royal palace.
Let all this city of Kadmos see, let them know you're here,
while I join my Bacchants in the clefts of Kithairon,
where their whirling dances await me
          now !

Exit DIONYSOS, *toward Kithairon.*

The CHORUS *enters from the direction of Thebes. They move rhythmically, to the beating of drums.*

CHORUS
     Out of Asia
          over Tmolos
               racing down
     we come
          crying *evohé* —
               Evohé O Bromios,
     Roaring god,
          you,
               you we serve
     with this labor
          the sweet

sweet labor
of crying
evohé
evohé unending
evohé
until we drop
evohé from joy.

Stand back, stand back
make way
hold your tongues
in holy silence
we sing
of sacred
everlasting things,
the blessings,
the song of Bacchus!

STROPHE

Blessed is he
who knows the rites
and consecrates his life
so wholly there
on the mountain
dancing his soul
over and into
the pack
of Bacchus.
Blessed are they
who can feel the awe
can celebrate Cybele
and move to the music
of the Great Mother's dance,
shaking the thyrsos
with ivy crowned
serving our lord,

Dionysos, *evohé*!
Come O Bacchae! Come
Bring down the god
the roarer
god born of thunder
god born of god
bring him down
down from the mountains
of Phrygia
down into Greece,
to Greece, to her cities,
dance Bromios
through her streets.

ANTISTROPHE

Bromios
born from lightning
in labor bitter,
a blast bolting
through her womb, the thunder
of Zeus clapping around her,
poor mother,
leaving this life
in childbed struck
by light
by a blow
from above.
But Zeus saved him
Zeus, son of Kronos,
his own son he saved
from the blaze
and buried him in his thigh,
bound him
with broaches of gold
away from the gaze
of Hera.

But then Zeus bore him,
>with a nod from the Fates,
>>birthed him
a bull-god
>and crowned him, his horns,
>>with coils of snakes,
beasts that we Maenads
>hunt and weave
>>through our hair.

STROPHE

O Thebes
>nurse of Semele
>>with ivy crown
yourself, explode into green
>everywhere sprout
>>with vines
creeping and clustering
>lush with flowers of white
>>and berries of red
Abandon yourself
>to the dances
>>danced with torches streaming
with glowing branches
>of cypress and branches
>>of oak.
Wrap yourself
>in fawnskin,
>>gird your dappled hide
with strands of snow-white wool
>that coil
>>with holy curls.
Dare it!
>Dare to be holy
>>holding the violent wand,
the sacred stalk

with its secret fire,
hold it
hold it and be holy
and suddenly
the earth
everything everywhere
is
in ecstasy exploding.
Bromios he is
whoever he is
who leads the god's pack
to the mountain,
to the mountain,
where all now await,
far away from their weaving
from shuttle and loom,
women now enthralled,
creatures possessed
by Dionysos possessed, *evohé*
evohé!

ANTISTROPHE

O Cave
of the Kouretes,
O Kretan cavern
O holy darkness
birth-
place of Zeus,
there Korybantes danced
beneath helmets triple plumed
around this primal drum
this skin whose pounding
mixed with shrill
Bacchic cries
and sweetly breathing
Phrygian flutes

a gift
for mother Rhea,
    the pulse
        that Bacchants beat to
chant to
    roar to,
        since the time
that frenzied Satyrs took
    the Mother's sacred drum
        in gift to the dancers
of the god's great year,
    the joy of Dionysos,
        evohé, evohé!

EPODE

O he is sweet
    upon the mountains,
        from the fast pack
he breaks and falls
    to the earth
        all wrapped in his fawnskin
falls upon a goat
    for the joy
        of its fresh blood
for the joy
    of its raw flesh.
        To the mountains
of Phrygia, to the mountains
    of Lydia he runs
        he is Bromios
who leads us
    evohé
        evohé!
Open earth and flow
    with milk
        with honey

with wine flow.
> The Bacchic one
>> is come
With blazing brand he runs
> trailing smoke
>> that spins the air
so sweet
> as sweet as frankincense,
>> darting here darting there
he rouses stragglers with his cries,
> stirs them with his dancing,
>> tossing back his handsome head,
flinging curls
> that stream behind him.
>> And above
all their shouts of joy
> you can hear him
>> roaring: *Come O my Bacchae! Come!*
with the glitter of Tmolos
> *that runs with gold*
>> *upon you, come,*
shine, sing for Bacchus
> *thunder out his worship*
>> *on your drums, all glory*
to the god, come crying
> *shouting, wailing*
>> *evohé,*
evohé!
> *let the holy flute*
>> *shriek with holy music*
let it lift you up
> *to those roaming*
>> *those running*
to the mountain
> *to the mountain,*
>> *where, like a foal*

feeding by its mother,
   my light-limbed Bacchant
     goes leaping for joy.

Enter TEIRESIAS *decked out as a Bacchant. He is an old blind man, and uses his thyrsos as a cane. An* ATTENDANT *leads him to the palace gates which he strikes with his thyrsos.*

TEIRESIAS

Look here! Does someone keep the gates?
Call Kadmos, son of Agenor, the Sidonian stranger
who built this towering city of Thebes.
Let someone go and tell him that Teiresias is here.
He'll know why. We have a pact, one old man to another,
to wrap our staffs and crown our heads with ivy
and deck ourselves in skins of fawn.

Enter KADMOS, *also in Bacchic regalia. He too is ancient and leans upon his thyrsos.*

KADMOS

Ah my old friend! I knew that voice of yours,
knew those words, so wisely spoken, must be yours.
Yes, I too am ready. See, I wear the costume of the god.
For I tell you, Teiresias, we must exhalt him,
exalt this god with all our strength. Why, he's the son
of my very own daughter, this Dionysos, and is now revealed
on earth, divine in the eyes of all mankind.

   So tell me Teiresias, where do two old men go
to tread this dance and toss their hoary heads?
You're the expert here. I tell you, I feel as if
I could beat the earth with my thyrsos day and night
and never tire. Oh, how sweet it is, Teiresias,
to forget we are old.

TEIRESIAS

Yes, I feel it too.
I too feel young — young enough to dance!

KADMOS

Then shall we take my chariot to the mountain?

TEIRESIAS

Better we should walk, it shows the god more honor.

KADMOS stretches out his hand to TEIRESIAS.

KADMOS

Come then, your hand, one old man shall lead another.

TEIRESIAS

Why, the god will lead us both, with no effort on our part.

KADMOS

Are we the only men who will dance for Dionysos?

TEIRESIAS

We alone, it seems, have sense. The rest are impious fools.

KADMOS

Then no more delay. Come, your hand.

TEIRESIAS

Here, take hold, together we go as one.

*The blind man gropes toward KADMOS until he finds his outstretched
hand.*

KADMOS

Yes, for I too am no more than
a man and dare not scoff at heaven.

TEIRESIAS
                   No, compared to gods
our wisdom is nothing — the weight of long tradition in this,
tradition as old as time, handed down from one generation to the next
and no argument, no matter how clever, can prevail against it.
To one who says I mock my age to go off dancing,
an ivy chaplet on my head, I say the god does not discriminate
young dancers from old, that he craves honor from one and all alike,
that no one — no one — is excluded from his worship.

KADMOS
                   Come, I'll be your eyes, Teiresias,
this once my words will be your guide.

> KADMOS *begins to lead* TEIRESIAS *slowly towards Kithairon. On the other side an* ARMED GUARD *suddenly appears. The old men turn toward them. Young and athletic in appearance,* PENTHEUS *hurries through the ranks.*

KADMOS
                   Why, there's Pentheus, Echion's child,
the boy to whom I gave my throne, and in some hurry too,
heading straight for the palace. He seems worked up indeed.
Let's wait, and hear what he has to say.

> PENTHEUS *stops in the center of the stage and wheels in anger, facing front.*

PENTHEUS
                   I heard
all about it, though I was away, far from this place,
still I heard of this new evil unleashed on our city.
Our women, they say, have left their homes, gone,
run off to hide in the mountains, bastard Bacchants
infatuated with this latest god, this Dionysos,

whoever he is. One thing's for certain, he fills their cups
and sends them slinking off, one by one, into the bushes
where they serve the lusts of men! Oh, but Maenads they claim to be,
why even Priestesses! Priestesses indeed! Priestesses of Aphrodite!
She is the god they serve, not Bacchus!
        Some I have already netted.
They are bound at the wrist and locked in the common jail.
The rest, like animals, I'll hunt them down from that mountain:

He points toward Kithairon.

Ino, Aktaion's mother Autonoe, even my own mother, Agave.
I'll throw them all in chains. I'll end these obscene rites of theirs —
now !
        I hear that a stranger,
some kind of shaman from Lydia, has come to town.
He has long, blond, scented hair, they say, and flushed cheeks
and the charms of Aphrodite darting in his eyes.
Day and night, they say, he tantalizes our young girls,
dangling his mysteries, promising them ecstasy
and the rapture of his initiation — but I can promise you this,
if I lay my hands on him inside these walls,
he won't be thumping that thyrsos or tossing back his head,
not when I've cut him off — at the neck!
        This is the very man now claiming Dionysos
is some god. From *him* comes that story
about Dionysos' being sown into the thigh of Zeus.
But make no mistake, Dionysos was burned to a crisp
by the same bolt that struck his mother
for lying about the bed of Zeus. I ask you,
shouldn't we string him up by the neck, this stranger,
whoever he is,
        imagine the audacity,
coming *here* adding outrage to indecency?

PENTHEUS *turns to enter the palace but stops, catching sight of* KADMOS
and TEIRESIAS.

PENTHEUS [*Cont'd.*]
> But what is this?
Will wonders never cease? Teiresias in dappled fawnskin!
And my grandfather — what's this, a joke of some kind? — shaking
a Bacchant's wand! Old father, it pains me to see you,
at your age, playing such a fool. Come now,
shake that ivy from your staff,
grandfather, put down that thyrsos!

> *Turning suddenly on* TEIRESIAS.

> It was *you* who did this, wasn't it Teiresias?
Yes, of course, you have given mankind yet another new god,
and yourself another opportunity to collect fat fees
for watching birds and reading signs. But believe me,
your grey hair alone saves you. Otherwise, you'd be in chains,
with other Bacchae — but this is outrageous!
How dare you bring these obscene orgies here!
Of only this, old man, can you be sure:
when women mix with wine, they glow — but not with holy light.
There's no mystery here.

CHORUS
> Profanity!
Oh Stranger, you know no shame before heaven,
before Kadmos who sowed the dragon's teeth!
Will you, the Snake-Man Echion's son, shame your own race?

> TEIRESIAS *raises his thyrsos, silencing the* CHORUS. *All eyes are now*
> *upon him. He fills the silence with an expansive gesture, then, in the*
> *direction of* PENTHEUS, *begins to speak.*

TEIRESIAS
> Give a clever man a good brief to plead   *comment about contemp. Athens*
> and eloquence is no great feat.
How smoothly the well-turned phrases come rolling off your tongue,
but there's little sense in what you say.

The man whose skill at speaking comes only from *conceit*
can prove a danger to his city, especially
if he acts the fool.
                    This "latest god," whom you now mock,
how great he will be through all of Greece, I can barely begin to say.
Mankind, young man, possesses two blessings ranked supreme:
first, the goddess Demeter, or call her Earth or whatever you like,
she is the dry principle sustaining human life.
But after her comes Semele's son, whose own gift matches hers:
the liquid life, the juice of the vine!
And when it flows, this juice,
it can release humanity from what afflicts it,
end our pains and give us sleep so sweet
that we forget the trials of our days. I tell you,
there exists no other medicine for misery like this.
And mark my words, this is the very god we pour in libation
to other gods, and so on *him*,
the favor of heaven itself depends.

        You sneer, do you, at that story
about Dionysos' being sown into the thigh of Zeus?
But let me teach you what this means:
From the flames Zeus snatched his newborn son
and brought him, a god, up to Olympos.
Of course, Hera contrived to throw the infant out of heaven,
and so Zeus devised a scheme, one well worthy of his godhead.
Out of the shining ether that encircles the world
he shaped a likeness, and being of ether
it shone in the sky like a god. *This* Dionysos
he handed over to Hera, a hostage for his son.
Now, after much time and many tellings, the story grew confused,
and people mixed up "shone" with "sown" and so
made up this other myth: the god who was "sown in the thigh"
for the god who "shone in the sky."
        I tell you, this god *is* prophecy, pure and simple,
he sends a madness, a frenzy that is prophetic.
Let him enter a man's body outright and

trying to rationalize the myths

the man he possesses will be endowed with future sight.
He is a warrior too, this god, being part Ares in his power.
Why, a whole army tensed and ready for battle
he can panic before it so much as lifts a spear.
Yes, this frenzy too comes from Bacchus. And soon,
you will see him high above the Delphic rocks,
with torches leaping from peak to peak, whirling,
shaking his Bacchic wand, a god worshiped everywhere,
great in Greece. Trust me, Pentheus,
brute strength is no match against power like this.
Whatever you think, your thoughts are unsound.
Don't mistake them for wisdom, Pentheus. No, you must
embrace this god instead, invite him into your land,
pour libations, dance his dance, put an ivy crown around your head.
    I will admit, Dionysos does not compel a woman to be chaste.
But as with everything else, chastity depends upon a woman's character.
If a woman is pure, the god's ecstasies cannot corrupt her.
    Look, you are pleased when crowds gather at your gates
so the city resounds with the name of Pentheus. Well,
the god delights in glory too, and so, Kadmos and I,
whom you think fools! will crown our heads with ivy
and dance in honor of this god — a pair of grey old men, it's true,
but dance we will and dance we must. Never, will your words convince me.
Never, will I war with gods. *That* is madness,
Pentheus, you put yourself at awful risk.
Truly, you are not well, and no drug can cure,
though surely some has caused, this sickness you now suffer.

CHORUS

Wise words Apollo would approve, old man,
wisely you honor Bromios: a god and great.

KADMOS

My boy, Teiresias counsels well. Your home is here,
with us, not alone, outside our laws.
Just now you're upset and not thinking straight.

Why even were this god, as you say, no god at all,
say he is one just the same. It's a noble lie:
our Semele mother of god, just think of the honor
it confers on our race.

   You saw what happened to Aktaion,
so sure he could outhunt Artemis, vaunting in her sacred grove!
By his own dogs he was torn to pieces, savaged by hounds
he'd raised from pups. No Pentheus, you mustn't, you mustn't
let this happen. Come, join us instead. Let me circle your head
with an ivy crown. Join us, show honor to this god.

   KADMOS *starts to move toward* PENTHEUS, *when abruptly ...*

PENTHEUS
   Keep your hands off me!
Go — go worship your Bacchus, if you like, but
don't touch me, I won't be infected with this idiocy of yours.
But by god, I'll make *him* pay, the man who taught you this.

   Turning quickly to his ARMED GUARD.

   One of you, go, *now*, take an ax
to his "prophetic seat," turn everything inside out,
smash it into a hundred pieces, destroy it all then
throw his holy ribbons out, expose them, prey to wind and rain.
Yes, *that* will make him burn.
   The rest go, comb the city for that
effeminate stranger who infects our women
with this strange disease and pollutes our beds.
And when you've got him, tie him up and bring him to me.
He'll find justice here in Thebes. We'll see he's stoned —
just as his Bacchus would wish — stoned to death in our streets.

TEIRESIAS
   You fool!
You have no idea what you're saying, before

you were unreasonable, but this is really madness,
raving madness.

      Kadmos, let us go, and pray
for this wild man and his city, pray that they
provoke the god no further.

The two men once again move off slowly toward Kithairon.

Come, follow me, put your weight on the ivy wand.
Support me with your other arm. That's it,
we'll hold each other up. Not a pretty sight,
two old men falling. No that wouldn't be right.
Yet go we must, go to Bacchus: it's the son of Zeus
we serve.

      But Kadmos beware,
lest someday your house repent of Pentheus.
No prophecy, just fact. The fool
has committed folly.

The old men exit from view. The CHORUS *begins to beat its drums and
then to dance.* PENTHEUS *remains, still as a statue, before his palace,
intently watching this spectacle.*

CHORUS

               STROPHE

Holiness,
    Queen,
        Holiness in heaven,
hovering over Earth
    on wings of gold
        have you heard
have you heard
    these words of Pentheus
        this outrageous attack
upon Bromios,
    upon Semele's son,

men
s

to merge with his dances
and laugh with his flute
	shaking off cares
		in the glow of the wine
at feasts of the gods
	is to know
		his mystery
his ivy crown
	is to feel
		his embrace
his
	holy
		sleep.

ANTISTROPHE

A tongue without reins
	a mind that knows
		no law
can only come
	to a bad end
		but a mind
at peace with life
	mindfully lived
		cannot be shaken
does not bring
	the house down
		in ruin.
From above
	they see all,
		these gods,

Use in paper

though they live
in a shimmering sky
far away from mankind.
Our wit is not wisdom
nor to think
thoughts more than human.
So briefly we live,
and who chases
after things too high
loses the little
he has here today.
But along this path run many,
many the mad and
many the fools
among mankind.

STROPHE

Away, take me away,
lead me off
to Kypros
isle
where Desires
enchant
the minds of men
where rivers,
fed by foreign streams
from hidden sources underground,
flow from a hundred mouths
and make the fields of Paphos
fertile,
take me away
away to where the Muses were born
and now sit in beauty,
those Pierian hills that climb
soar to solemn Olympos, *there*
O take me *there*

me *there* to your dances,

     es,

and *there* Desire,

    there your rites

are righteous

    there your Bacchae

     blessed!

ANTISTROPHE

This god, this spirit, this

    son of Zeus

     takes joy

in feasting, joy in abundance,

    joy in the goddess Peace

     whose gift to the young

is joy

    the joy of Life itself.

     To rich and poor alike

he gives the wine

    that gives us pleasure

     that numbs our pain.

But to the man

    who turns away

     from a life rich

by day and blessed by night

    with simple joys like these,

     to the man whose mind

edges the gods in heaven,

    he turns

     a very different face.

To us,

    give humble thoughts,

     no more

than most

    would think

     is right.

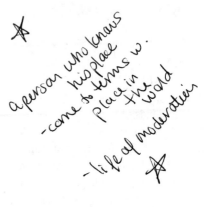

A person who knows his place — come to terms w. place in the world

— life of moderation

The GUARDS *enter with their bound prisoner, the* STRANGER *with the smiling mask.* PENTHEUS *rushes forward to meet them.*

GUARD

We have him, Pentheus, we stalked him

[handwritten: hunting imagery]

just as you said. See, our hunt was successful.

But sir, I must confess, this wild beast you sent us after
was, well, quite tame. In fact, he offered no resistance
and attempted no escape. He just stood there, offering his hands,
and never blanching. No, his cheeks were flushed,
as though with wine, and smiling he bid us bind him,
making our job, sir, well embarrassingly easy.
I told him I felt ashamed. "Listen, stranger," I said,
"I do this against my will, my orders come from Pentheus."

But Pentheus, those Bacchae that you clamped in chains
and shut behind bars are free, *gone*, bounding away
across the meadows shouting for their god, shrieking *Bromios!*
Out of nowhere, chains broke and fell from their legs
and bolts shot from the doors — not the work of human hand!
Full of wonders, Pentheus, comes this man to Thebes ...
but what happens next, of course, is up to you.

PENTHEUS

Untie his hands, he's netted now,
he won't be dancing out of this ...
Well, you're quite beautiful, aren't you?
Or so women must think, now don't they?
Here in Thebes, at any rate,
which is why you've come.

PENTHEUS *moves toward and then circles his prisoner. He begins to fondle his hair.*

What a mane of hair you have! So long and lovely!
Look how it tumbles down your cheeks, what hand-holds

[handwritten: refers to his hair in a sexual sense]

Fondling more aggressively.

for a wrestler! And such white skin, just look.
How fastidious you must be! Keep it from the sun?
Prefer the darkness, do you? Oh yes, so much better
for hunting Aphrodite with your beauty.
                    But enough. Your race, stranger?

DIONYSOS

Nothing to brag of and easy to tell.
You've heard of Tmolos, the mountain steeped in flowers?

PENTHEUS

                    Yes.
It encircles the city of Sardis.

DIONYSOS

                    I come from there.
Lydia is my home.

PENTHEUS

                    Then why Greece?
Why bring these rites to Thebes?

DIONYSOS

                    Dionysos,
the son of Zeus, has brought me.

PENTHEUS

                    Zeus?
Some Lydian Zeus who spawns new gods?

DIONYSOS

                    The same Zeus
who married Semele, *there.*

Pointing to the smoldering altar.

PENTHEUS

> Then he forced you,
> face to face, or in a dream?

DIONYSOS

> He *gave* me his rites,
> seeing that I could see.

PENTHEUS

> These rites of yours,
> what form do they take?

DIONYSOS

> It is forbidden
> to tell a man who does not believe.

PENTHEUS

> Then tell me this,
> what do those who sacrifice hope to gain?

DIONYSOS

> I am forbidden to say,
> but it's worth knowing.

PENTHEUS

> And you're clever,
> at making me curious.

DIONYSOS

> No. All is clear.
> The mysteries of god abhor the godless man.

PENTHEUS:

> This god you say you saw,
> what form did he take?

DIONYSOS

Whatever he wished.
It wasn't for me to say.

PENTHEUS

Another evasion
and more nonsense.

DIONYSOS

Sense seems nonsense always
to a fool.

PENTHEUS

Are we your first victim,
or did you bring this god to other lands?

DIONYSOS

Barbarians everywhere
now move to his mysteries.

PENTHEUS

Barbarians!
They are more easily moved than Greeks.

DIONYSOS

In this, a wise move:
their ways are different.

PENTHEUS

These mysteries,
are they performed by day or by night?

DIONYSOS

Mostly by night:
the awe is greater then, in darkness.

PENTHEUS

And for women
greater chances for deceit and things still more disgusting.

DIONYSOS

By daylight too
there is cause for disgust.

PENTHEUS

You!
You will be punished for these smart remarks!

DIONYSOS

And you,
for your impious stupidity toward the god!

PENTHEUS

Well, what a bold Bacchant!
You wrestle well, with words.

DIONYSOS

Yes, so tell me
the terrible things you have in mind?

PENTHEUS

First,
I'll cut those luscious curls of yours.

DIONYSOS

My hair is holy.
I grow it for the god.

PENTHEUS *draws his sword and cuts the god's hair.*

PENTHEUS

Now the thyrsos.
Give it to me.

DIONYSOS

You take it.
I carry it for Dionysos.

PENTHEUS *seizes the thyrsos.*

PENTHEUS

And now you
I'll throw in chains.

DIONYSOS

The god himself
will free me, whenever I wish.

PENTHEUS

Wish away,
you'll find no Bacchus without your Bacchae.

PENTHEUS *gestures and the* GUARDS *position themselves opposite the*
BACCHAE.

DIONYSOS

But he is here now and sees what I suffer.

PENTHEUS

Indeed, where? Or have my eyes gone blind?

DIONYSOS

Here, with me. And yes, your blasphemy
blinds you.

PENTHEUS *turns to his* GUARDS.

PENTHEUS

Take him!
He mocks me and Thebes!

DIONYSOS

Don't touch me!
Be warned: you're out of control.

PENTHEUS

I'll show you who's in control!
Seize him, I say!

DIONYSOS

You do not know
what you do, nor who you are,
nor why you live.

PENTHEUS

I am Pentheus,
born of Agave and Echion!

DIONYSOS

You will live to repent that name.

PENTHEUS

Take him away. To the stables. Lock him in.
If it's the dark he wants, give him darkness.
Go dance in there.

The GUARDS *bind* DIONYSOS' *hands and the* BACCHAE *beat their drums
with growing agitation.*

And these women,
your accomplices in making trouble here,
I'll sell them as slaves, or put them to work
at my looms. *This* will keep their hands
from drumming.

DIONYSOS
> I go, though not to suffer
what cannot be. But Dionysos whom you outrage,
whom you deny, will punish you for this.
Chain me and it's to him you're bound.

The GUARDS *lead* DIONYSOS *off.* PENTHEUS *follows. With ferocious energy, the* CHORUS *now begins to dance.*

CHORUS
                              STROPHE
Dirke,
> holy Dirke,
> > virgin daughter,
born from the waves,
> of Achelöos,
> > O sacred spring,
once you held him,
> fast in your waters,
> > Dionysos
saved from the flames
> and sown in the thigh
> > of his father,
Zeus the immortal
> who hailed him
> > *twice-born son,*
Dithyrambos, come!
> *Be hidden here,*
> > *in the hollow*
of my male womb!
> Let Thebes hear this,
> > O twice-born Bacchus,
let it know you
> let it name you now
> > by the wonder of your birth!

O Dirke,
    holy Dirke,
        why now
do you drive me
    and my women
        crowned with ivy
away,
    away from your waters
        and the feel
of your sweet streams?
    Why?
        Why deny me?
Why expel me?
    Still you must care
        you must
care for Dionysos,
    shining in his clusters,
        for the sweet wine
glowing in his grapes,
    still
        for Bromios
you must!

ANTISTROPHE

Do you see
    Do you see
        what rage
this earth-spawned
    dragon-seed
        son of Echion,
this Pentheus,
    now vaunts
        against heaven?
Not a man,
    but an earth-born beast
        he is

some dragonish thing
    with death
        roaring wild in his eyes,
a giant revolting
    against the gods on high!
        Even now he dares
throw ropes
    around this body
        that to Bromios belongs
and dares
    throw my friends down
        in the dark of his dungeons.

Do you see this,
    Dionysos, son of Zeus,
        your prophets all
trapped in a struggle
    for life?
        Come, soaring down
from Olympos
    come striking, shake that
        golden flashing thyrsos
crush the outrage
    of this deadly man
        this beast of blood.

EPODE

O Dionysos
    where do you lead
        the dancers who dance
with your thyrsos?
    To Nysa,
        to the mountain mother
of all wild things
    or the peaks
        of Korykos?

Or maybe deep,
    deep in the woods
        of Olympos
where beasts
    lay their lairs,
        where once Orpheus sang
to his lyre
    and made music so sweet
        that the trees grew wet
with weeping
    and wild beasts
        grew tame.
O Pieria,
    mountain mother of Muses,
        you he adores,
you he honors,
    the one they call
        Evohé!
Evohé he will come
    leading his dancers!
        And nothing will stop him
stop him or his revelers
    through rivers he leads them
        he whirls them
he spins them, his Maenads
    go wading
        through Axios roaring,
through Lydia glistening,
    through bliss-giving waters
        that make our land of horses
gleam —

    From offstage a sound, inhumanly deep, like the bellow of a bull.

DIONYSOS
> *Hear me, O my Bacchae,*
> > *hear*
> > > *this is my cry.*

> *Again, the eerie sound. The* CHORUS *looks wildly in every direction.*

CHORUS
> What is it?
> > ·This cry
> > > that calls us?

DIONYSOS
> *Again I call you.*
> > *It is I,*
> > > *son of Semele, son of Zeus!*

CHORUS
> O lord, O master
> > come to us
> > > O Bromios come!

DIONYSOS
> *Come Earthshaker god,*
> *shake the floor of this world!*

> *A deep rumbling thunder. The palace starts to shake. Slightly at first,*
> *then as if struck by an earthquake. The* CHORUS *trembling and crying*
> *out singly.*

CHORUS
> — Look! It moves, the palace of Pentheus is shaking!
> — Pieces are falling!
> — Soon the whole thing will collapse!
> — He is here! Dionysos is here in this house!
> — Honor him!
> — Bow to him!

— Look, *there*, the front columns are trembling
— Up *there* look, the main beam is cracking
— Look out, it's about to come crashing down!

With a violent jolt the stone architrave cracks in two and flies off the pillars supporting it, hurtling to the ground. It shatters into pieces with a loud peal, followed by a roar from within.

CHORUS
— Listen, it's him, it's Bromios roaring inside those walls.

DIONYSOS
Strike lightning, burn fire, blaze!
Torch the house of Pentheus!

A bolt of forked lightning strikes the house and the tomb, which bursts into flames, followed by a loud crash of thunder. The palace fills with smoke. The CHORUS *runs in all directions, crying out with terror.*

CHORUS
— Do you not see?
— Yes, with my own eyes I see it
— Fire streaking over Semele's tomb
— The flame Zeus left himself
— The lightning he hurled with his thunder
— O throw your trembling bodies down
— Down on the ground, Maenads, bow low
— For look he now comes, he is here,
— The son of Zeus, our lord
— He will bring this high house
        down!

The CHORUS *prostrates itself and salaams toward the palace gate. Through the smoke a dim figure emerges — the* STRANGER *in his smiling mask. He picks his way lightly through the rubble and then walks in mock solemnity toward his prostrate followers.*

DIONYSOS

Ladies, my Lydian ladies, what is this?
Were you afraid? What, so overcome by fear
you threw your bodies to the ground? Why,
you act as if you'd seen Bacchus himself
pounding the palace of Pentheus. But come now,
stand up, come on, up up up. Be brave.
Courage now, I'll not have you lumps of quivering flesh.

Seeing their leader, the CHORUS *rises.*

CHORUS

O greatest light! O leader of dances!
To see you is such relief. We thought we were lost.

DIONYSOS

You lost heart, you mean, when they led me in?
Did you think I'd stay put down there,
in those dreary dungeons?

CHORUS

What else could we think?
And if anything happened to you, where could we turn?
But how did you escape that godless man?

DIONYSOS

Quite easily.
In fact, I freed myself with no effort at all.

CHORUS

But how?
Didn't he use ropes to tie up your hands?

DIONYSOS

Yes, and even in this
did I abuse him. I let him think he tied me up, but he never so much

as touched me. No, he held me — only in his dreams. You see,
in the very stall where he'd left me and thought he'd locked me in,
he found a bull and around its hooves and knees he threw his ropes,
panting with rage, his body dripping sweat, biting his lip,
while I sat by serenely watching.

    But then came Bacchus to smash the house
and ignite the blaze in his mother's tomb.
And Pentheus, seeing this and thinking his house on fire,
grew frantic, dashing this way and that, ordering his servants,
Water, bring water, the whole Acheloös if need be!
In they ran, every slave working like mad, and all, of course, for nothing.
But Pentheus, afraid I might escape, gave up this bucket brigade
and charged back inside, black sword waving in his hand.
And there in the courtyard, Bromios fooled him with a phantom,
or so it seemed, I can't be certain, but Pentheus certainly thought
it was me, and eager for my blood, he rushed it, stabbing at the shining air.
But enough, thought Bacchus, time he was humbled — punished
severely as he deserves. And so you see, just look,
there lies his house, a heap of rubble on the ground.
Bacchus brought his palace down, smashed it to pieces,
he let Pentheus see what trouble he was bound for
when he threw those ropes on me.

    Now beaten and weary, he drops his sword.
About time! Imagine: a mere man, nothing more,
who dares do battle with god!

    For my part, I left the palace quietly,
and worry no more about Pentheus.

            But wait, I think I hear him, yes,
the stomping of boots inside. Any second he'll rush out here.
What, I wonder, will he say? No matter, I will take him
lightly, though he come on snorting fire. The wise man
always shows a restrained and even temper.

PENTHEUS *comes running forward, breathless and bewildered, fighting his way through the rubble.*

PENTHEUS

Outrageous! This is outrageous! The stranger is gone!
I had him, he was *mine*, bound in chains,
but somehow he slipped me ...

Seeing him suddenly, PENTHEUS *gasps in amazement.*

Good god! This is the man! But how! How are you here,
in front of my house? Did you walk right through ...

PENTHEUS *starts toward the* STRANGER.

DIONYSOS

Hold it, not another step, I warn you, Pentheus,
tread lightly.

Unsure, PENTHEUS *keeps his distance.*

PENTHEUS

                But how did you get out?
How could you slip through chains?

DIONYSOS

                Did I not say —
or did you not hear — that someone would free me?

PENTHEUS

Who? You're always playing on words, always!

DIONYSOS

The one who makes the grapevine grow for men.

PENTHEUS

You mean the one who meshes the minds of men.

DIONYSOS

Saying this, you damn what Dionysos deems his glory.

From Kithairon, a MESSENGER *appears.* PENTHEUS *wheels on him and gives an order.*

PENTHEUS

Go immediately! Go, I tell you, shut the gates
at every tower, close the city tight!

Uncertain, the MESSENGER *remains frozen.*

DIONYSOS

Why? Can a god not walk over walls?

The STRANGER *steps lightly over a piece of the fallen facade.*

PENTHEUS

You're clever, very clever, but not
when and where it counts.

DIONYSOS

No, when and where it most counts,
in this wise, born wise. But you ...
Pentheus, at least listen to this man, at least hear him out.
He comes from Kithairon with some news.
And I shall wait right here. Don't worry,
I promise, I won't run away.

The MESSENGER *makes a deep bow and, straightening himself, begins.*

MESSENGER

Pentheus, king of Thebes,
I come from Kithairon, where snow forever
falls in glistening shafts of white, where ...

PENTHEUS

Is your message urgent?

MESSENGER

I've seen the Bacchae! Those wild women who shot
like arrows from this city, barefoot and crazed,
their long white legs streaking in the air.
And I come here, lord, wanting but to tell you
and tell this city the things I have seen,
things strange and terrible these women do,
more miracles than marvels, truly. But first,
may I speak freely, or must I guard my speech?
I fear your quick temper, lord, and that
all too royal passion running in your blood.

PENTHEUS

Speak. I will not harm you in any way.
One cannot begrudge an honest man. But,

Pointing at the STRANGER.

the more terrible your stories about the Bacchae
the more terrible my justice against *this man*
for teaching our women all these tricks.

MESSENGER

Our cattle had climbed to the crest of a hill
where the grazing was good and sun's first rays
came streaming down, warming the earth.
And there, in this light, I saw them,
three bands of Bacchic women:
One led by Autonoe, another by your mother,
Agave, and a third by Ino. They were sound asleep,
bodies sprawling everywhere, some with backs braced
by boughs of pine, while others, scattered here and there,
slept wherever they happened to fall, nestled in among the oaks,
with piles of leaves for pillows. A picture of modesty it was,
not as you say, women off in the woods alone, drunk with wine
stalking Aphrodite to the cooing of flutes.

But all of a sudden, awakened by the lowing of our bulls no doubt,
your mother stood up in the middle and cried out — *ololu* —
to rouse her Bacchae. And rubbing sleep from puffy eyes
they sprang to their feet — and that was a sight
to behold: women, young and old alike, even girls,
all moving like one, a picture of calm, of loveliness itself!
First they shook their heads and let their hair fall loose
across their shoulders. Those whose straps had slipped
tied up their dappled fawnskins and girt them round
with coiling snakes who licked their cheeks.
New mothers abandoned babies to take up fawns
and wolf cubs in their arms and give these wild creatures milk
that oozed from swollen breasts. As one they donned their crowns
of ivy, oak, and evergreen.
A rock one struck with her thyrsos sprang a fountain
of water clear as dew. Another drove her wand in the ground
and there, at the touch of the god, rushed wine.
To get milk they just scratched the earth barehanded
and the white drink came spurting up in streams. And down
the ivy thyrsos tip dripped a thick, golden flow of honey.
I tell you, had you been there, Pentheus, your protests
would turn to prayers, seeing what this god can do.
      Now we cowherds and shepherds gathered in groups
to compare our stories of these miraculous sights,
when this stranger, a smooth talker from town, suddenly called on us all:
You highland men who call these majestic mountains home,
what do you say, shall we hunt Agave, mother of Pentheus,
flush her from the Bacchic pack and win the favor of our king?
Well, sound advice it seemed, so we withdrew and laid an ambush
in the undergrowth. At the appointed hour,
the Bacchae waved their wands and began their revel,
crying with one voice *Iakchos, Bromios, son of Zeus!*
Then a shudder and the whole mountain moved,
as if everything suddenly went wild with god,

the Bacchae bolted and beasts bolted too.
Nothing escaped this sudden surge.
    It happened that Agave ran close by where I was hiding,
so I leaped out in the hope of capture, but spotting me
she started shouting *O my swift hounds, look,*
we are hunted here by men. Come, follow me,
your wands are now your weapons!
    Well, we didn't wait around. We fled and barely missed
being torn to bits by the Bacchae. Down on the meadow they swooped
and attacked the grazing herd barehanded.
Here one woman lifts a fat calf,
still bellowing with fear, and pulls it apart with her hands,
there the pack descends shredding cattle to pieces, flinging
hooves, ribs, everywhere flying, and flesh dripping blood
now hangs from the trees. Furious bulls, rage rising in their horns,
are suddenly slammed to the ground
gripped by a hundred clawing girls and flayed alive
more quickly than you can blink your royal eyes.
Off they fly like birds, running so hard
their feet barely touch the plain, speeding
past those fields by the Asopos that grow Thebes its corn.
Like an invading army they rush down on Hysia
and Erythia in the foothills of Kithairon
and plunder all they find.
Even children they seize and set up on their shoulders,
where their loot stays propped without ropes! Not even bronze,
or iron falls — nothing so much as grazes this dark ground.
And fire dances in their hair, flames that do not burn them.
But so incensed were those townsmen the maenads plundered
they came out to battle the Bacchae with arms,
and this, my lord, was a dreadful sight,
the men's pointed spears cut no flesh and drew no blood,
but when those women threw their wands they made blood flow
and put that army of men to flight — some god,
I tell you, was *in* them.
Then back they went to where they began,
those springs the god's touch made flow,

and there they washed off gore, while snakes
licked the blood that dribbled from their cheeks.
     This god, lord, whoever he may be, accept him here in Thebes.
He is great in many ways. This same god, they say,
gives mankind the plant that can ease his pain.
And without wine, where would we find love,
or Aphrodite, or anything else that brings us joy.

CHORUS

I shudder to speak in the tyrant's presence,
but let it be said: there is no god
greater than Dionysos.

PENTHEUS

             Like a fire out of control
this Bacchic violence spreads. It comes too close.
We are disgraced in the eyes of Greece. Let's move!

Turning toward the MESSENGER.

Go at once to the Electran gates, and order out my forces.
Tell the cavalry I want their best troops and fastest horses,
summon my archers, every man who can string and pull a bow,
tell them all we march against the Bacchae! It's gone too far,
when we endure such things at the hands of women!

DIONYSOS

Nothing, Pentheus, have you learned, nor even heard
a single word. Still you abuse me, but still I warn you:
do not take up arms against a god, go easy, Pentheus.
Bromios will not let you force the Bacchae from this mountain
that echoes with his cry.

PENTHEUS

            You've broken free of your chains,
is that not maddening enough? Or will you preach too
and drive me madder still? Shall I throw you back again?

DIONYSOS

Sacrifice would I perform
not sacrilege commit. You're a man. He's a god.
Only an ass kicks against a whip.

PENTHEUS

Ah yes, a sacrifice:
I'll see that the blood of many women darkens Kithairon's glades,
as they deserve.

DIONYSOS

You will not touch them.
They will disgrace you, their Bacchic wands will turn
your shields of bronze around.

PENTHEUS

This stranger is impossible.
He leaves me tongue-tied. In chains or out,
nothing shuts him up.

DIONYSOS

Friend,
still you can set things right.

PENTHEUS

Doing what?
Enslaving myself to my slaves?

DIONYSOS

Without bloodshed,
I will lead the women home.

PENTHEUS

Oh yes,

as if wheels of trickery do not spin against me here.

DIONYSOS

How so,
if I offer to save you by my own devices?

PENTHEUS

How so!
You've made an eternal pact with your master of revels.

DIONYSOS

Yes,
I've made a pact, but with god.

PENTHEUS suddenly turning again to the MESSENGER.

PENTHEUS

Go!
Bring my armor here!

Turning to the STRANGER.

And *you,* not one more word.

He turns abruptly and starts for his palace when a strange sound stops him dead in his tracks.

DIONYSOS

AAAAAAAAAAAAAAAAAAAAAAAAAAAAAAAAAAAAAAAAAH!
Would you like to see them, huddled up there,
on the mountain?

PENTHEUS turns around slowly as if in some kind of trance.

PENTHEUS

See?
I'd give much gold to see that sight.

DIONYSOS
>   Why this sudden change?
> This is what you now desire?

PENTHEUS
>   But it would pain me
> to see them drunk and out of control.

DIONYSOS
>   But you'd like to see this,
> you'd like it, even though it caused you pain?

PENTHEUS
>   Yes, yes,
> I could hide beneath the pines.

DIONYSOS
>   But they can track you down,
> sniff you out even though you hide.

PENTHEUS
>   Openly then, I'll go openly.
> Everything you say is true.

DIONYSOS
>   Then shall I lead the way?
> Will you put yourself in my hands?

PENTHEUS
>   The sooner the better,
> let's waste no more time.

DIONYSOS
>   Then a linen dress,

first you must put one on.

PENTHEUS

What?
Will I end up looking like a woman?

DIONYSOS

They'll put an end to you,
if you go there looking like a man.

PENTHEUS

You've spoken well again,
like someone who's known for some time ...

DIONYSOS

I have a good teacher,
Dionysos has taught me all I know.

PENTHEUS

Then tell me what to do,
so that all works as you've planned.

DIONYSOS

First, I must help you dress.

Gesturing toward the ruined palace.

Let us step inside.

PENTHEUS

Wait.
Did you say a *dress?* A *woman's* dress? But I'll die of shame!

DIONYSOS

Perhaps,
you no longer desire to see the Maenads?

PENTHEUS

No, I mean yes.
But first tell me what I must wear.
　DIONYSOS *walks slowly in a circle around* PENTHEUS, *as if sizing him up.*

DIONYSOS
We'll have to do something with your hair.
You'll have a long, flowing wig.

PENTHEUS
Yes, just like yours.
And what next?

DIONYSOS
A dress, ankle length.
And a band to hold back your curls.

PENTHEUS
Is that it?
Isn't there more?

DIONYSOS
There is indeed.
You must carry a thyrsos and wear the spotted fawnskin.

PENTHEUS
But what if I can't go through with it,
I mean, dress like a woman?

DIONYSOS
It's that or pay with blood,
if you battle with the Bacchae.

PENTHEUS
No, you're right,
I must spy on them first.

DIONYSOS

        Much wiser
than hunting bad with worse.

PENTHEUS

        But the city of Kadmos,
how will I pass through it unseen?

DIONYSOS

        Along deserted streets,
I will lead you.

PENTHEUS

        Anything is better
than to be mocked by the Bacchae.
I think I'll sort this out inside,
and there decide which way seems best.

DIONYSOS

Of course. I'm ready whatever you decide.

PENTHEUS

Well then, in I go, and either I march in arms
or do as you advise.

    PENTHEUS *walks off into the remains of his palace.* DIONYSOS *watches him go and then turns to the* CHORUS.

DIONYSOS

O my women we have him, he thrashes in our net!
He goes to the Bacchae and there meets his death.
    Dionysos, you cannot be far now, the rest is yours.
And O make him pay, punish him for madness with madness
swiftly sent, drive him utterly out of his mind.

Sane he would never endure this, being dressed like a woman.
But possess his soul and he will put that costume on.
And for those threats that made him sound so fierce,
let him cut a womanly figure led through the city streets,
laughingstock of Thebes!
                    But go I must now and lay out the things
that down to Hades he will take, loved to death in his dear mother's arms!
He will learn that Dionysos, born of Zeus, is divine indeed,
a god most terrible to mortals — and most gentle too.

Smiling, DIONYSOS *exits into the palace. The* CHORUS *begins dancing and beating its drums.*

CHORUS

STROPHE

Will I dance
        and dance again soon!
            Will I,
whirling
        barefoot through the night,
                throw back my head
in the damp dawn air
        and the pale dawn light?
            Will I frisk
like a fawn at play
        in the green joy
                of the meadow,
a fawn
        who has fled
                from the chase
overleaped all the nets
        left behind her now
                far away
where the baying still drones
        way back in the distance,

        the hunters still driving
still urging their hounds.
    With a burst
        she is gone,
bounding away,
    vaulting the river
        she darts free
of man.
    In the joy
        of a dark wood
she plunges
    and fuses with the forest
        of leaves.

REFRAIN

What is wisdom?
    Or should we ask,
        what is right?
What gift from the gods
    is more righteous
        than the sight
of your hand held high
    above the head
        of an enemy?
What is right
    has always
        something of beauty.

[handwritten annotation: – not Platonic wisdom –]

[handwritten annotation: – here wisdom is an act of surrender to the Gods]

ANTISTROPHE

It rises slowly,
    the strength of god,
        but rises true
and punishes those
    who honor
        stupid pride,
or praise the mind unhinged

and decry the things of god.
      Secretly, subtly,
slowly it comes,
    the force of god
        in the foot of time
to crush the unholy.
    No,
      no one can know,
can live by
    laws greater than this.
      It costs us so little
to find strength here:
    what is strong is divine
      what lasts through time,
law sanctioned by nature,
    forever and always
      divine.

REFRAIN

What is wisdom?
    Or should we ask,
      what is right?
What gift from the gods
    is more righteous
      than the sight
of your hand held high
    above the head
      of an enemy?
What is right
    has always
      something of beauty.

EPODE

Blessed is the man
    who escapes
      from the storm at sea

and finds his
>> harbor.
>>>> And blessed the man
who can rise
>> above his burdens.
>>>> Fortune holds one man up
in different ways
>> above another.
>>>> Ten thousand are the shapes
of hope.
>> Some men find them
>>>> and live their lives in joy,
from others
>> they just slip away.
>>>> Blessed the man
who lives with joy,
>> Blessed the man
>>>> who lives for today.

[handwritten margin note: anti-Platonic — here it states, do sexual pleasures, drink wine etc.]

Out of the ruined palace walks DIONYSOS, *his smile unchanged. Only now, a bullish double walks beside him. He calls back after* PENTHEUS *who remains within.*

DIONYSOS
>Pentheus, O Pentheus, why still inside? I thought you were eager
>to see what you shouldn't and do what you daren't.
>Time to come out now, Pentheus, let me see your
>new look. Now what might you be? Woman, Maenad, Bacchant?
>Ah yes, the perfect disguise for spying on your mother and her pack?

>PENTHEUS *enters, walking gingerly, as if unsure of himself, or in some
>kind of trance. He is led by the god's bull twin, with the god beside
>him.* PENTHEUS *wears a long, linen dress which comes down to his an-
>kles. Over his shoulders and girdled about his waist is the Bacchant's
>fawnskin. Long, yellow curls fall across his shoulders. His resem-*

...nce to the god is uncanny. Only his mask displays, in place of the god's smile, the tragic actor's gape.

DIONYSOS

Well look at this!
Like a daughter of Kadmos, you are one and the same!

PENTHEUS *gazes in every direction, as if seeing the world for the first time.* DIONYSOS *and the bull creature stand side-by-side.*

PENTHEUS

Look! Two suns! And two Thebes! I see
two cities with seven gates each! And look,
look at you, leading the way, now a bull
you seem to be! With horns sprouting on your head!
But, were you a beast before? Now you are
a bull for sure.

DIONYSOS

The god walks beside us.
Before he was not your friend, but now
he is your ally. You see the things you should.

PENTHEUS

Well, how do I look? Am I not the image of Ino,
or perhaps my mother, Agave?

DIONYSOS

Looking at you,
it's like seeing them. But look here,
a hair has already fallen out of place.
That's not how I fixed it behind your band.

PENTHEUS

I must have shaken it loose inside when I was dancing,
throwing my head back and forth like this.

PENTHEUS *starts to demonstrate.*

DIONYSOS

Here. Let me be your maid and fix it for you.
But please, you must hold still.

DIONYSOS *steps toward him and begins to fix his hair, then stands back to scrutinize him with great disapproval.*

PENTHEUS

You dress me. I'm in your hands.

DIONYSOS

Now your belt's come undone and just look at your hem,
it must lie evenly across your ankles.

PENTHEUS

Yes, it's down on the right.

As DIONYSOS *hikes his dress on the right and tucks it into his girdle,* PENTHEUS *looks over his shoulder at the back of his left leg; he bends his left knee slightly and raises his heel.*

But look, on this side it falls just above my heel.

DIONYSOS *steps back to admire his creation.*

DIONYSOS

Much better, and when you've seen these Bacchae,
how modest they look, not wild as you've heard,
you'll think me the best friend you have.

PENTHEUS *shakes his thyrsos in his left hand.*

PENTHEUS

Do I do it like this, or with the right hand?
I will look just like a Bacchant!

DIONYSOS

In the right hand always, and raise it, like this,

DIONYSOS *demonstrates.*

first with the right foot up, then the right foot down.

PENTHEUS *follows.*

DIONYSOS

Yes,
I do commend this change of heart.

PENTHEUS

The cliffs of Kithairon,
Bacchae and all, have I the strength
to lift them up on my shoulders?

DIONYSOS

Yes, if you wish.
Before your mind was unsound. But now,
you think as you should.

PENTHEUS

Will we take spikes,
or shall I put my shoulders to the cliffs
and tear these mountains up with my hands?

DIONYSOS

But the haunts of the Nymphs,
the holy places where Pan plays his pipe,
you wouldn't destroy these?

PENTHEUS

No, you're right.
No need to use brute force on women.
I'll bury my body beneath the pines.

DIONYSOS

Yes, you'll find the ambush you deserve,
creeping up to spy on the Bacchae.

PENTHEUS

Yes, I think I see them already,
like mating birds in the bushes, trapped in the toil of desire.

DIONYSOS

Exactly what you must watch for.
You may surprise them — or they may surprise you.

PENTHEUS

Lead me away,
through the heart of Thebes. Let all see:
I alone dare do these things.

DIONYSOS

And you alone
will suffer for your city — you alone.
Such trials await you as you, and only you, deserve.
Follow. I will escort you safely there,
but another will lead you back.

PENTHEUS

My mother, you mean?

DIONYSOS

With you, an example to all men ...

PENTHEUS

Is it for this I go?

DIONYSOS

Oh you will be carried …

PENTHEUS

Such luxury …

DIONYSOS

… home in your mother's arms …

PENTHEUS

You'll be the death of me …

DIONYSOS

Yes, I mean to be.

PENTHEUS

I go to my reward.

DIONYSOS

An awe-inspiring man! Ordeals, awesome and awful, await you.
Your fame will climb the skies …
Stretch out your hands,
Agave and you other women of that same Kadmian seed.
I lead a young man to a great trial, in whose triumph
both Bromios and I will rejoice. But the rest,
the event will show.

With the bull creature at his side, DIONYSOS *leads* PENTHEUS *off in the direction of the city, which he will parade him through. Then, to Kithairon. The* CHORUS *now dances — with a vengeance.*

CHORUS

STROPHE

To the mountain,
to the mountain

    run
bitches of madness
    race to the place
        where the women of Kadmos
now hold their dances,
    go on goad him
        drive him deeper
into his madness,
    the man who looks
        like a woman,
the man who's looking
    for Maenads.
        But let his mother
see him first,
    crouched
        on smooth rocks
or perched in a pine,
    let her see him
        spying
and shout to her Maenads
    A hunter has come
        to the mountain
to the mountain he comes
    stalking the hills
        for the daughters of Kadmos
he comes.
    O Bacchae,
        who?
Who bore him?
    Not from woman's womb
        he comes,
this beast,
    he is some lion's whelp,
        some
thing spawned,
    a creature

from Gorgon's blood.

REFRAIN

Come Justice,
    let me see you now
        sword in hand
stabbing down
    through the throat
        that goddless
lawless
    reckless
        earthborn Echion's son.

ANTISTROPHE

With indecent thoughts
    and violent rage
        by a crazed mind
he is forged
    to make this mad assault
        to molest your mysteries,
Bacchus — you —
    and the mysteries
        of your mother,
he thinks to beat
    by force
        a god
that cannot be beaten.
    Deranged, derelict man
        he does not know
that Death
    will not give way
        will not be fooled
because he dares
    go against god.
        No!

Only live
    like a man
       and Life
brings less pain.
    Wisdom I don't envy.
       To seek,
to hunt
    is enough,
       and to rejoice
in things that are seen
    and touched,
       to live a life
that is pure,
    holy by day,
       holy by night,
at war with injustice,
    living by laws
       that honor the gods.

REFRAIN

Come Justice
    let me see you now
       sword in hand
stabbing down
    through the throat
       that godless
lawless
    reckless
       earthborn Echion's son.

EPODE

Now be
    revealed
       a bull now
be revealed
    a dragon

be with deadly heads
revealed a lion
> *be*
>> *with tongues of flame!*
Come O Bacchus
> *cast your deadly net*
>> *around the man*
who hunts your Bacchae,
> *catch him pouncing*
>> *on your Maenad pack,*
come O lord,
> *now let us see you*
>> *smile!*

A SECOND MESSENGER *enters from Kithairon.*

SECOND MESSENGER
How blessed this house once was in the eyes of Greece,
this land of the Snake where Kadmos came, a Sidonian stranger,
to sow the earth with a dragon's teeth!
Today, I mourn your end. I was merely your slave,
and now, losing as you do, am something less than this.

CHORUS
What's this? Some news of the Bacchae?

MESSENGER
Pentheus is dead. The son of Echion is no more.

CHORUS
O lord Bromios,
> a god you are,
>> and great!

MESSENGER
What are you saying? How can you rejoice

at the death of my master?

CHORUS

Not of your kind
    I shrill
        with barbarian song.
Never again
    will I tremble
        in fear of your chains.

The women shriek, a piercing, yelping, trilling cry.

MESSENGER

Do you think Thebes has no men …

CHORUS

Dionysos controls me
    Dionysos
        not Thebes!

MESSENGER

Then you might be forgiven — but to rejoice
at atrocities like these can never be right.

CHORUS

Then say,
    tell us
        his fate.
Was he not
    a reckless man
        plotting reckless ways?

As he speaks, the MESSENGER*'s gestures grow as graphic as his words.*

MESSENGER

We put the outlying villages and the river Asopos

behind us and struck into the foothills of Kithairon,
Pentheus and I — for I followed my master — and of course
that stranger who offered to be our guide.

Climbing, we found a dell and there lay in the tall grass,
not making a move or saying a word, hoping to see without being seen.
Just below was a hollow cut from the sheer rock,
steep cliffs rising around it and water rushing down to a swelling stream.
And there in the middle sat the Maenads, in the shade of a pine grove,
plying their hands at work that clearly gave them delight.
Some wove ivy crowns on wands that lacked these tips of power.
Others sang out of pure joy, spirited as fillies who've shed
their traces, trilling Bacchic cries that echoed
up and down the mountain. But, poor Pentheus, could not see
this riot of women, and said to the stranger, *Squatting here,*
I can barely make these bastard Bacchants out. But look,
if I could climb that pine overhanging the edge,
I could see their shameless orgies better.

At this the stranger did something stranger
than I had ever seen before: he took hold of that tree,
a tree so tall its branches pricked the heavens,
and made it bend. Drawing it slowly
down
    down
        down
          slowly
till the tip of the skyline branch
touched the black ground.

Like a giant bow it curved,
or a rim bent around a lathe. Just like that,
with bare hands, he bent that mountain pine
to the earth — the work of a more than mortal hand.
Then holding the tree to the ground, he seated Pentheus
on the topmost branch and with a slow, steady hand,
released the tree, taking pains that Pentheus not be thrown.
And so it rose, my master on its back, towering
high as heaven in the steep mountain air.

Then it happened: they saw him, the Maenads, and not he them.
Pentheus became visible, but only just, when the stranger vanished,
and out of the ether came some voice, it seemed the voice of Dionysos
roaring, *Look, my youthful women, look up here at what I bring you,*
a man who mocks at you and me and at my mysteries.
Punish him for that smile!
As this voice thundered, a bolt of awful fire blazed
and towered straight from earth to the height of heaven.

    The high air was still, dead silence hung in the glen,
not a leaf stirred, no animal made so much as a sound.
Straight up they stood, the Bacchae, stunned
by what they'd heard, straining their eyes in every direction.
Again he called them, and now they knew their master's cry.
Like birds they flew across the valley,
Agave and her sisters and the whole Bacchic pack,
running on legs that barely seemed to touch the ground,
bounding over swollen rapids, leaping over massive rocks —
the breath of god was in them. And when at last they saw my master,
perched way up on the pine, they climbed a towering rock
then battered him with branches and threw stones so hard
they singed the air. Thyrsoi filled the sky,
but no one hit him — poor Pentheus, perched there,
such a pathetic target — he was still above their throws,
but he was trapped, with no way out. Like thunder striking
they splintered oaks and heaved and hacked the pine,
prying the roots with wooden stakes, but every effort failed.
Still he hung there, helpless, high above them, till Agave spoke,
Come Maenads, circle round this trunk, take hold,
catch this climbing beast or he'll expose the dance of god!
A thousand hands then closed and tore that tree
straight out of the ground. And from way, way up, he plunged straight down,
hurtling to the earth with chilling cries — poor Pentheus,
he knew his end was near.

    His own mother was on him first, a priestess of sacred horror
on the verge of holy murder, when Pentheus tore the band from off his hair
that she might see his face and spare him. He touched her cheeks,

screaming, *No, mother, no, I am Pentheus, your son,*
the child you bore to Echion. Mother please, I have done wrong,
but you mustn't kill me for this!

In the corners of her mouth ran foam, and her eyes
spun in their sockets, so utterly out of her mind
in the grip of Bacchus, she could not hear him. He was god-
forsaken. She grabbed his left arm, just below the elbow,
and, putting her foot against his ribs, tore off his shoulder —
with ease. The god had put inhuman power in her hands.
Shredding flesh, Ino made short work of his other side,
soon Autonoe and the rest managed to get their claws in him.
Screams came from every mouth, even Pentheus groaned
with what little breath was left, and the Bacchae raised their bloody cry.
One woman marched off holding an arm, another held up a foot
still warm in its shoe. The body had been flayed, a carcass
clawed to the bone. Hands dripping blood, the women tossed
a chunk of Pentheus' flesh around as if it were a ball.

Now the body lies in pieces, scattered everywhere:
strips hanging from sharp rocks, gory bits lost in the leaves
of the forest floor. To find it again will not be easy.
But his head, you will see this soon enough: His mother has it,
and holds it high, impaled on her thyrsos like a lion's head!
She has left her sisters on the mountain with the Maenads
and marches in triumph through the foothills of Kithairon
and now comes *here*, inside these walls, exulting
in her catch — her *curse* — calling out for *Bacchus,*
fellow hunter, stalker of the kill, bringer of triumph —
triumph of tears.

I will leave this house before she comes,
and leave this tragedy behind me. With the gods,
prudence and reverence is best. If a man knows this,
he has, I think, all the wisdom he ever needs.

The MESSENGER *exits, away from Kithairon. The* CHORUS *exults in tri-*
umph.

CHORUS
Lift your feet
    up for Bacchus,
        and your voice,
lift it high
    in shouts full of joy
        for the death
dealt to Pentheus,
    spawn of dragon seed!
        Dressed like a woman,
a Bacchant,
    power-tipped
        wand of sure death
in his hand,
    he was led
        by a bull
to the end.
    Kadmian Bacchants,
        you have earned this triumph!
you deserve these tears!
    Your stakes were high
        and now a mother's arms
are stained
    with the blood
        of her son.

From Kithairon, AGAVE *enters dancing with* PENTHEUS' *head impaled on her thyrsos. Her steps match those of the* CHORUS. PENTHEUS' *long, yellow hair and hanging tendrils are matted with blood. The* CHORUS *stops dancing when they see her.*

        But look, there she is,
the boy's mother rushes toward us; her eyes read madness.
Greet this maenad dancer who steps to our Lord of Cries.

AGAVE *charges the* CHORUS, *holding up the head. They are stunned,*

and then, somewhat reluctantly, as if from sympathy, allow AGAVE *to
lead them in her victory dance.*

STROPHE

AGAVE
Asian Bacchae! LOOK!

CHORUS
Why must you urge me?

AGAVE
On my thyrsos
look at these tendrils
newly cut,
from the mountain,
a god-send
this catch.

CHORUS
So we see.
We greet you,
fellow Bacchant.

AGAVE
A young lion,
with bare hands
I caught this
savage creature.
Here!
Look and see!

AGAVE *thrusts forward the grisly head.*

CHORUS

Caught in the wilds?

AGAVE

On Kithairon ...

CHORUS

On Kithairon?

AGAVE

... this beast was killed.

CHORUS

But who killed him?

AGAVE

I struck him first.
Agave the blessed
I am called by my pack!

CHORUS

Any others?

AGAVE

Kadmos ...

CHORUS

Kadmos!

AGAVE

His daughters,
but only after *me*
after *me*,
did they touch him,
only after me!
Look, look
how blessed I am

in *this*,
my catch!

ANTISTROPHE

Come!
share in the feasting!

CHORUS

What,
poor woman,
should I share?

AGAVE

See,
this cub is young,
look
beneath his mane
are cheeks that bloom
with soft
new hair.

CHORUS

Yes,
like a wild beast
he looks
with that mane.

AGAVE

A skillful hunter
is Bacchus.
With skill
he whirled his Maenads
on this beast.

CHORUS

Yes,

he is Lord
of the hunt.

AGAVE

You praise me then?

CHORUS

I praise you.

AGAVE

Soon all Thebes ...

CHORUS

Even Pentheus, your son ...

AGAVE

... will praise his mother,
the huntress,
          captor
of this lion's head!

CHORUS

A prodigy!

AGAVE

Yes!
A prodigal catch!

CHORUS

Exalted,
    Agave?

AGAVE

I am over-
    joyed.
Greatness,
    greatness shines

in such spoil!

AGAVE *lifts her trophy high and, dancing, shakes it up and down in triumph.*

CHORUS
Yes, now show the city this spoil you bring,
poor woman, display your trophy to Thebes.

Turning toward Thebes.

AGAVE
Come citizens of towering Thebes, come see
this beast that we, the daughters of Kadmos, snared,
and not by throwing spears of bronze or casting nets,
but with only *these* — our long, white nails.
What is all your boasting worth, you men
who take an arsenal out to hunt, when women
can catch a beast like this and tear him limb from limb
with nothing but bare hands!
      Where is my old father? He should be here!
And Pentheus, my son, where is he? Let him bring a scaling-ladder,
and climb it, rung by rung, till he reach the roof-beams,
and *there* nail up this head, this lion on which I preyed!

Enter KADMOS *from Kithairon.* ATTENDANTS *follow carrying a litter. On it are the piecemeal remains of* PENTHEUS, *covered by a shroud. They move somberly across the orchestra without seeing* AGAVE.

KADMOS
Come, follow me, bring in your heavy burden,
the body of Pentheus, found only after what seemed
an eternity of searching, scavenging over the back of Kithairon,
where it lay scattered, everywhere, hidden
beneath an impenetrable wood.

Old Teiresias and I had already left the mountain
and come as far as these city walls when I heard
of this monstrous thing my daughters did. And so,
to Kithairon I returned and now bring this child,
by Maenads murdered.
I saw them, the Bacchae still there on the mountain:
Autonoe, once herself a mother — of poor Aktaion — and with her Ino,
both still in the woods and still plagued with madness.
Agave, they say, now marches here, dancing insanely for Dionysos.

KADMOS sees AGAVE for the first time. He stumbles backwards.

     Ahh! Agave!
So it's true, and this truly a god-
forsaken sight.

AGAVE sees KADMOS and approaches him with trophy held high.

AGAVE

Father, now you can boast to the world,
you have sired daughters greater by far
than other mortals — all of us, father,
but me above all. I left my shuttle by the loom
and climbed to greater things, like catching beasts
barehanded!

She removes the head from the thyrsos and cradles it.

And just look here, in my arms I hold the prize,
the glory of our hunt. I bring it home to you,
to hang up there upon your house. Here, hold it, father.
Reach out your hands. Come, exult in my hunting,
call all your friends to a feast! A blessing,
a blessing, father, have I showered on you
by these feats.

The old man staggers back and averts his eyes.

KADMOS

        This is more than my eyes can bear!
This is grief beyond enduring! A blessing, you call it!
Blood, blood is what you've showered on us all,
the blood that stains your hideous hands.
A feast, a feast you bid me attend!
Oh a fine sacrifice you have made to the gods!
I can offer only tears, tears for you, and then for me.
This god has had his justice, if you call this justice:
Lord Bromios, god of our blood, killer of his kind.

AGAVE

        Bile runs in your veins,
old man, not blood, bile turns your look so black!
If only my son were a hunter, if only he took my example
and led young men of Thebes in the chase after prey.
But that boy! Fighting with god is all he can do!
He needs a word to the wise, father, and needs it from you!
Who will call him here? He must see me just like *this*,
when the gods are with me, in this, my moment of glory.

   With a groan, KADMOS *slowly turns to* AGAVE.

KADMOS

        If ever you know
what you have done, you will grieve, and terribly grieve.
But if you remain, forever, as you are now,
then count it your fortune not to know your misfortune.

AGAVE

        Grief,
when I feel glory, no, I don't understand.

KADMOS

        Your eyes,
turn them toward the ether, stare straight at the sun.

She flings back her head.

AGAVE

There,
what should I see?

KADMOS

Things around you,
do they seem the same, or changed from before?

AGAVE

Brighter,
things seem clearer, less hazy than before.

KADMOS

That shiver,
do you still feel it in your soul?

Starting at KADMOS.

AGAVE

No,
I don't know what you mean ... I feel somehow
calmer, as though my mind were somehow changing.

KADMOS

My voice,
can you hear it now, can you answer clearly?

AGAVE

You know,
I've forgotten, father, what we were just saying.

KADMOS

On your marriage day,
to whom did I give you?

AGAVE

To Echion,
a man, they say, who sprang from the dragon's tooth.

KADMOS

And your son?
What son did you bear your husband?

AGAVE

Why Pentheus,
born from the love I bore his father.

KADMOS

In your arms now,
whose head do you hold?

AGAVE

That of a lion,
or so the hunters told me.

KADMOS

Now look closely.
A glance is all it will take.

*She looks at her hands, transfixed by the head with long, blood-mat-
ted hair, disfigured almost beyond recognition.*

AGAVE

What am I seeing?
What could this thing be?

KADMOS

Look hard at it.
You know what you see.

Scream. Then through sobs.

AGAVE

Yes,
I see a grief so great it has no name.

KADMOS

The head of a lion
you no longer see?

AGAVE

No, it is —
the head of Pentheus I hold —

Followed by wailing.

KADMOS

Mourned by me
long before you saw him.

AGAVE

Who killed him —
why is he in *my* hands?

KADMOS

O savage truth,
to come just now!

AGAVE

Tell me!
My heart is pounding against my sides?

KADMOS

You killed him,
You and your sisters.

AGAVE

But where?
Here by the house, some other place?

KADMOS

The very place
the hounds tore Aktaion to pieces.

AGAVE

Kithairon?
What possessed Pentheus to go there?

KADMOS

The god
he went to mock, and you in your ecstasy.

AGAVE

My ecstasy?
Was I held there by some spell?

KADMOS

Madness,
you and all the city were possessed.

AGAVE

Now too late, too clearly I see,
Dionysos has destroyed us!

KADMOS

You abused him,
denying he was god.

AGAVE

My precious child,
father, where is his body?

KADMOS *points to the litter.*

KADMOS

Over here,
though much was lost ...

AGAVE

His limbs,
could you join them, could you make him whole?

Slowly KADMOS *lifts the shroud. It is a gory sight: dismembered limbs
and flesh patched over stomach and ribs — beneath the heap of
bloody pulp, the outline of a human form. Silence, followed by a cry.*

Why! Why! Why was Pentheus punished for crimes
that were mine?

KADMOS

Like you,
he disdained the god. And so with one blow,
the god smites us all: you and him, and *in him*, my house.
Now I have no heir, no male child. Look there,
this branch of your own body cut down, dying a horrible,
inhuman death — this boy, like the light of day in my house,

KADMOS *kneels.*

you, child, child of my child, you were our support,
you stood like a pillar in my halls and struck awe
abroad in the city; no one who'd ever met your eyes
dared insult my age. They knew too well the price
they'd pay. But now I, Kadmos the Great,
will be an exile, polluted, driven from my home.

I who sowed the whole race of Thebes now reap a grim harvest.
This boy, he was to be our bloom, our stem, our root.
O my most lovely child, of all men always you were dearest,
and always will I love you still, dead no less than alive,
but now your hand

His face pressed against the body.

                will never touch my cheek again,
nor will you ever hold me and call me *Grandfather,*
and ask me, *Has anyone wronged you, old man,*
has anyone shown you anything less than respect?
Who has troubled you, father, tell me?
Who has made your old heart hurt? Tell me
and I will punish him soundly, my old father,
you whom none may mistreat.
      But now I am broken, and you suffer what must be past
all enduring, you, his mother, you and your sisters.
And if any man still despises gods, let him look at this,
at the death of this boy; let him believe in gods then.

CHORUS

Kadmos, I am moved by what you suffer: your grandson
got the justice he deserved, but his death bears hard on you.

    AGAVE *now kneels beside the body. She emits a shrill, keening cry*
    and begins a dirge over the body of her dead son. In her hands she
    still cradles his head.

AGAVE

O father, yes it bears hard on you, but look
look at me, look at the creature I have become ...

    Suddenly, overhead a dragonish thing. It is leonine with bulging eyes
    and a Gorgon's mane of snakes around its head. From its mouth, be-
    tween two long fangs, hangs a flamelike tongue of red.

DIONYSOS

A dragon will you be and your wife bestialized
like you will be transformed into a serpent:
so much for your divine marriage to Harmonia,
daughter of Ares — mortal!
With her at your side, you will drive a chariot drawn by bulls,
as the oracle of Zeus decrees, leading deadly armies against Greece,
and many will be the cities that fall beneath your numberless
barbarian hordes. When at long last,
they plunder the shrine of Apollo, back you will go
again beating a miserable retreat.
But, in the end, Ares will save you and your wife,
and send you to spend the rest of your days
in the land of the blessed.

Mark my words, I am not from mortal born,
but born from Zeus!
Temperance!
You gave no thought to it, but had you
shown me signs of sanity sooner,
you might have known my blessing
and found the son of Zeus your friend.

KADMOS

Dionysos,
please, I beg you, you have done us wrong!

DIONYSOS

Too late!
You knew me too late, the damage was done.

KADMOS

We have learned.
But your justice goes too far.

DIONYSOS

Too far!

I, a god, was outraged by the likes of you!

KADMOS

A god indeed!
Then why act in anger like a man?

DIONYSOS

These things!
They were decided long ago by Zeus, my father.

AGAVE

It's finished, father,
we are exiles, all.

DIONYSOS

Then why delay?
Your yokes await you.

AGAVE *lays the head of* PENTHEUS *beside his body. Slowly, she and* KADMOS *rise, turning toward one another.*

KADMOS

My child, the end we have come to — every one of us,
you and your sisters and I — fills me with dread.
Nor is it over. More horrors will come.
Imagine me, an old man, exiled to barbarian lands,
doomed to lead a grisly army against Greece,
and my wife, Harmonia, the child of Ares,
changed like me into a dragonish fiend,
marching beside me and the armed hordes I bring
to destroy the graves and altars of Greece.
And this evil will never end, not ever,
not even when I have gone down infernal Acheron
will I find any peace.

A bloody embrace.

AGAVE

O father,
to go like this into exile without you!

KADMOS

Poor child,
why hold me so, the way a swan
throws its wing around its gray,
grounded father?

AGAVE

Where will I go,
father, now without a home?

KADMOS

I don't know.
Your father can help no more.

AGAVE

Then farewell
house of Kadmos,
farewell
my ancestral city,
I leave you
for a worse fate
exiled
from my bridal bed
and my home.

KADMOS

Go now,
child,
join poor Aristaios,
the father
who saw Aktaion

die.

AGAVE

For you I grieve most, father.

KADMOS

And I for you, daughter,
for you, and your sisters.

AGAVE

Brutally
has Dionysos
brought disaster
on this house.

DIONYSOS

Brutally
did I suffer
at your hands,
my name
abused
by Thebes.

AGAVE

Father, farewell.

KADMOS

And farewell
to you, poor child.
Fare well.
But you will find
your faring hard.

KADMOS *now turns to go. Alone, he leaves by the way he came, back toward Kithairon.* AGAVE *calls to his* ATTENDANTS *who watch him disappear.*

AGAVE

Lead me to my sisters,
　　my sisters in sorrow
　　　　and the exile to come.
I will go anywhere,
　　so long as I never see
　　　　Kithairon,
that hill so unholy
　　with blood,
　　　　take me anywhere
so long as Kithairon will never see me,
　　and no traces of thyrsoi
　　　　are anywhere to be found.
I leave these
　　to other
　　　　Bacchants.

The ATTENDANTS *lead* AGAVE *off. Only the* DRAGON GOD *above, the*
CHORUS, *and the body below remain.*

CHORUS

Many
　　are the forms
　　　　of god.
Much
　　that is strange
　　　　they do.
What we expect,
　　does not happen.
For what we don't,
　　the god finds a way.
And so it happened,
　　here.

[handwritten annotation:] anti-Platonic — anything can happen from Gods doesn't have to be rational

CLASSICAL TRAGEDY:
Greek and Roman

Eight Plays accompanied by Critical Essays
Edited by Robert W. Corrigan

" A KNOCKOUT!... PROVOCATIVE... BOLD... READ-
ABLE... STAGEWORTHY..."
—**Timothy Wiles**, Author, *The Theatre Event*
Indiana University, Professor of English

paper • ISBN: 1-55783-046-0

CLASSICAL COMEDY:
Greek and Roman

Six Plays accompanied by Introductions
Edited by Robert W. Corrigan

"I know of no other collection of Greek and Roman plays
as valuable to theatre departments."
—**James M. Symons**, President, Association for
Theatre in Higher Education

paper • ISBN: 0-936839-85-6

ANTIGONE
by Bertolt Brecht

A Play
With selections from Brecht's Model Book
Translated by Judith Malina

Sophocles, Hölderlin, Brecht, Malina — four major figures in the world's theatre — they have all left their imprint on this remarkable dramatic text. Friedrich Hölderlin translated Sophocles into German, Brecht adapted Hölderlin, and now Judith Malina has rendered Brecht's version into a stunning English incarnation.

Brecht's *Antigone* is destined to be performed, read and discussed across the English-speaking world.

paper • ISBN: 0-936839-25-2

CUSTOM OF THE COUNTRY

Based on Edith Wharton's 1913 novel
Adapted by Jane Staton Hitchcock

This brilliantly crafted stage version of Wharton's sprawling novel dissecting the New York social scene focuses on the beautiful, but predatory, Undine Spragg and the men in her life.

Representing a world motivated by a heartless desire for power and status, Undine takes on lovers and husbands, discarding them when her whims of iron move her.

"A Luminous Adaptation" — THE BOSTON GLOBE

Performance Rights available from Applause Theatre & Cinema Books

$6.95 Paperback
ISBN: 1-55783-287-0

APPLAUSE

AN ACTOR'S DICKENS:

Scenes for Audition & Performance from the works of Charls Dickens

Adapted and Edited

by Beatrice Manley

Beatrice Manley has selected 80 scenes from various Dickens classics, providing as well, background information, a discussion of the character's emotional temperament, and a short summary of events that lead into the selected scene. This book for the first time allows actors to play Dickens in the unmatchable original. It is a useful guide for the classroom as well as for the actor training to capture the magic of Dickens, whether in an audition, on the movie screen, or on the stage.

Paper•ISBN 1-55783-469-5 • $10.95

The Scarlet Letter
by Nathaniel Hawthorne

Adapted for the stage by
James F. DeMaiolo

Leslie Fiedler pronounced it the first American tragedy. F.O. Mathiessen considered it the "Puritan Faust." Richard B. Sewall compared its inexorable dramatic force to King Lear. These chieftains of American literature were not, as one might suspect referring to a play by O'Neill. They are not in fact, referring to a play at all, but to a masterpiece of nineteenth century fiction. Until now, it appeared that Nathaniel Hawthorne's haunting drama of judgment, alienation and redemption would be forever confined to the page. The Scarlet Letter continues to be the most frequently read novel in American high schools today as well as one of the most widely circulated novels in the American library system. And now comes the stage version to do it justice.

A century and a half after its first incarnation, James DeMaiolo has forged an alliance of craft and spirit so potent in its own right and so faithful to Hawthorne's original that his stage version is certain to compel all non-believers to recant and take heed. The audience joins the chorus as they weigh the American contract of freedom against the fine print of convention and taboo.

Paper • ISBN 1-55783-243-9 • $6.95
Performance rights available from APPLAUSE

MEDIEVAL AND TUDOR DRAMA

Twenty-four Plays
Edited and with introductions
by John Gassner

The rich tapestry of medieval belief, morality and manners shines through this comprehensive anthology of the twenty-four major plays that bridge the dramatic worlds of medieval and Tudor England. Here are the plays that paved the way to the Renaissance and Shakespeare. In John Gassner's extensively annotated collection, the plays regain their timeless appeal and display their truly international character and influence.

Medieval and Tudor Drama remains the indispensable chronicle of a dramatic heritage — the classical plays of Hrotsvitha, folk and ritual drama, the passion play, the great morality play *Everyman*, the Interlude, Tudor comedies *Ralph Roister Doister* and *Gammer Gurton's Needle*, and the most famous of Tudor tragedies *Gorboduc*. The texts have been modernized for today's readers and those composed in Latin have been translated into English.

paper • ISBN: 0-936839-84-8

The Day the Bronx Died

A Play
by Michael Henry Brown

"THE DAY THE BRONX DIED COMES ON LIKE
GANGBUSTERS...LIKE A CAREENING SUBWAY TRAIN
spewing its points in a series of breathless controntations"
—MICHAEL MUSTO, *The New York Daily News*

"Michael Henry Brown is A SMOKING VOLCANO OF A
WRITER...THE DAY THE BRONX DIED is an engrossin
drama... the danger exceeds our expectations"
—JAN STUART, *New York Newsday*

Two childhood friends—one black, the other white—
struggle to live in a racist world.

Michael Henry Brown wrote the screenplay, DEAD PRES-
IDENTS directed by the Hughes brothers. He is the author of
the HBO Mini-series LAUREL AVENUE. Among his other
plays is GENERATION OF THE DEAD IN THE ABYSS OF
CONEY ISLAND MADNESS which was produced to great
acclaim at the Long Wharf Theatre in New Haven and the
Penumbra Theatre in St. Paul

Paper•ISBN 1-55783-229-3 • $6.95

Performance rights available from APPLAUSE

❦APPLAUSE❦

BEST AMERICAN SHORT PLAYS 1998-1999

The Likeness by THEODORE APSTEIN • Home by LAURA CAHILL • Fifteen Minutes by DAVE DECHRISTOPHER • No Crime by BILLY GODA • I Dream Before I Take The Stand by ARLENE HUTTON • Reverse Transcription by TONY KUSHNER • Jade Mountain by DAVID MAMET • What Drove Me Back to Reconsidering My Father by JOHN FORD NOONAN • Deux-X by JULES TASCA • Boundary County, Idaho by TOM TOPOR • All About Al by CHERIE VOGELSTEIN

$15.95 • PAPER • ISBN: 1-55783-429-6 • $32.95 • CLOTH • ISBN: 1-55783-425-3

BEST AMERICAN SHORT PLAYS 1997-1998

Belly Fruit by MARIA BERNHARD, SUSSANAH BLINKOFF, JANET BORRUS • Little Airplanes of the Heart by STEVE FEFFER • The Most Massive Woman Wins by MADELEINE GEORGE • The White Guy by STEPHEN HUNT • Time Flies by DAVID IVES • The Confession of Many Strangers by LAVONNE MUELLER • OEDI by RICH ORLOFF • Creative Development by JACQUELYN REINGOLD • The Man Who Couldn't Stop Crying by MURRAY SCHISGAL • The Trio by SHEL SILVERSTEIN

$15.95 • PAPER • ISBN 1-55783-426-1 • $32.95 • CLOTH • ISBN 1-55783-365-6

BEST AMERICAN SHORT PLAYS 1996-1997

Misreadings by NEENA BEEBER • The Rehearsal: A Fantasy by J. RUFUS CALEB • The Vacum Cleaner by EDWARD de GRAZIA • Mrs. Sorken by CHRISTOPHER DURANG • Four Walls by GUS EDWARDS • I'm With Ya, Duke by HERB GARDNER • My Medea by SUSAN HANSELL • I Didn't Know You Could Cook by RICH ORLOFF • Tunnel of Love by JACQUELYN REINGOLD • Fifty Years Ago by MURRAY SCHISGAL • Your Everyday Ghost Story by LANFORD WILSON • Wildwood Park by DOUG WRIGHT

$15.95 • PAPER • ISBN 1-55783-317-6 • $29.95 • CLOTH • ISBN 1-55783-316-8

PAUL SILLS'
STORY THEATER:

Four Shows

Adapted for the stage
by Paul Sills

**Including essays and introductions by
Paul Sills on directing for *Story Theater*
and
A Special Section: Theatre Games for Story Theater by
Viola Spolin**

The creator of Story Theater, the original
director of Second City, and one of the great
popularizers of improvisational theater, Paul Sills has
assembled some of his favorite adaptations from world literature:

The Blue Light And Other Stories
A Christmas Carol - Charles Dickens
Stories of God - Rainer Maria Rilke
Rumi - Jalalludin Rumi

CLOTH•ISBN 1-55783-211-0 • $26.95
Performance rights available from APPLAUSE

WOMEN HEROES
Six Short Plays from the Women's Project

Edited by Julia Miles

The English Channel, the United States Government, Hitler, cancer—these are a few of the obstacles which these extraordinary women hurdle on their way to ticker tape parades, prison cells and anonymous fates.

COLETTE IN LOVE Lavonne Mueller
PERSONALITY Gina Wendkos & Ellen Ratner
MILLY Susan Kander
EMMA GOLDMAN Jessica Litwak
PARALLAX Denise Hamilton
HOW SHE PLAYED THE GAME Cynthia L. Cooper

paper • ISBN: 1-55783-029-0
$8.95